PATHS TO THE RIVER BANK

And a River went out from Eden

The sketch by Graham Robertson which was the only illustration to appear in the first edition of The Wind in the Willows, published in 1908.

PATHS TO THE RIVER BANK

The Origins of
The Wind in the Willows

From the writings
of Kenneth Grahame
and Introduced
by PETER HAINING

Illustrated by Carolyn Beresford

SOUVENIR PRESS

Copyright © 1983 Peter Haining

First published 1983 by Souvenir Press Ltd,
43 Great Russell Street, London WC1B 3PA
and simultaneously in Canada

ISBN 0 285 62565 9

Printed in Great Britain by
Ebenezer Baylis & Son Ltd,
The Trinity Press, Worcester, and London

FOR
My children, Richard, Sean & Gemma
– to keep them company with
Mole, Rat, Badger & Toad

Contents

RUNNING WATER

Water brown, water bright –
   Pearls and swirls that sever;
Running water's my delight
   Always and for ever;
Let it from the chalk go peep,
Let it from the limestone leap,
Let it off the granite steep
   Pour, or from the mill be;
Sunshine's daughter,
Running water
   Was and ever will be.

A poem by Kenneth Grahame
written at Blewbury in 1915.

Introduction

"For every honest reader there exist some half-dozen honest books which he rereads at regular intervals of six months or thereabouts. Whatever the demands on him, however alarming the arrears that gibber and grin in menacing row, for these he somehow generally manages to find time. Nay, as the years flit by, the day is only too apt to arrive when he reads no others at all; the hour will even come, in certain instances, where the number falls to five, to four – perhaps to three."

These words were written by Kenneth Grahame in 1895, some dozen years before he gave the world just such an "honest" book as he described here, *The Wind in the Willows*. Grahame might well have stretched his point even further, for there are people of my acquaintance who read *only* that classic tale of the adventures of Mole, Rat, Badger and Toad, year in and year out, each time finding something new in its rich, effortless prose which conjures up in a magical and quite unique way the aroma of the English countryside and the lives of its small denizens. Like a breath of Spring, the book can be picked up as the dark and cold of Winter begin to fade into memory, and when finished it stands like an open door into Summer. No one I know has ever read *The Wind in the Willows* and been quite the same person afterwards.

Whenever I think of the book I am instantly reminded of Mole, at the very opening of the story, freeing himself from the drudgery of spring cleaning and wandering along the river bank, bewitched by the glories of nature all around him. "By the side of the river he trotted," Kenneth Grahame writes, "as one trots,

when very small, by the side of a man who holds one spellbound
by exciting stories; and when tired at last, he sat on the bank,
while the river still chattered on to him, a babbling procession of
the best stories in the world, sent from the heart of the earth to be
told at last to the insatiable sea.''

Grahame knew and understood and wrote about nature and
wildlife with such brilliance that it is no wonder his book has
survived for three quarters of a century (it was first published in
1908); nor that it has kept its author's name evergreen for fifty
years since his death early on the morning of July 6, 1932, at his
home close to the River Thames at Pangbourne. Generation after
generation, young and old, have indeed felt like that child trotting
alongside Grahame himself, while he holds us spellbound
recounting the dramas of the inhabitants of the river bank.

Kenneth Grahame loved animals with a consuming passion
and came to write his materpiece about a group of them because
of a deep-seated conviction that he *owed* them something. Late in
his life he confessed, ''As for animals, I wrote about the most
familiar and domestic in *The Wind in the Willows* because I felt a
duty to them as a friend. Every animal, by instinct, lives according to his nature. Thereby he lives wisely, and betters the
tradition of mankind. No animal is ever tempted to belie his
nature. No animal, in other words, knows how to tell a lie. Every
animal is honest. Every animal is straightforward. Every animal is
true – and is, therefore, according to his nature, both beautiful
and good. I like most of my friends among the animals more than
I like most of my friends among mankind.''

When one considers the life of Grahame, his creation of a book
such as *The Wind in the Willows* seems all the more remarkable.
Born in Edinburgh in 1859, he seemed destined for a long and
distinguished career in banking: joining the Bank of England as a
clerk in 1879, and becoming its Secretary in 1898. Only ill-
health, it is said, prevented him seeing out his days in the august
surroundings of Threadneedle Street. There were hints, however,
that although he was a dedicated and conscientious servant of the
City, his mind on occasions wandered to other things. He loved
to escape from London and wander for hours along the Thames

Valley or across the rolling landscape of Berkshire and Oxfordshire. He was equally fascinated by childhood and the fantasy
worlds of children. Writing had come quite naturally to him since
he was a boy, and so he began to amuse himself in his spare time
by writing essays for the London magazines. Several of these
"little meteorites", as he called them, were rejected, but as he
was not driven by any financial necessity to sell them, he merely
shelved the failures and continued writing as the fancy took him.
What these early essays did reveal was that Grahame clearly
possessed an eye for the ways of nature and the countryside as
well as a remarkably subtle, delicate and humorous sympathy
with the minds of children. It was almost as if he had never grown
up; as if his mind were still tuned in to the way children reacted to
the world around them, grown-ups in particular. He was able to
express their thoughts as if he were still one of them, and not in
the way that an adult *believed* they thought. Though he is often
mistakenly categorised as a children's writer, Kenneth Grahame
actually saw his readership as adult, and accessible as his work is
to the young, it none the less demands the closest attention from
any age group if it is to achieve the greatest effect.

The bulk of the tales which Grahame wrote during this period
found their way into two collections, *The Golden Age* (1895) and
Dream Days (1898), and it is a startling fact that these works,
plus an earlier slim volume of essays, *Pagan Papers* (1893),
constitute, with *The Wind in the Willows*, the sum total of his
output. With the exception, of course, of most of the pieces in this
book. (Perhaps just for completeness sake, I should add that he
also wrote a small number of poems, also uncollected.)

Writing of the first two collections, Graham Robertson, a
close friend of the family and the designer of the frontispiece (and
only illustration) for the first edition of *The Wind in the Willows*,
has said:

"Anyone who wants to know Kenneth Grahame may still find
him in *The Golden Age* and *Dream Days*, the eternal boy, keenly
alive to the beauty and wonder of the world around him, yet shy
of giving expression to the strange happiness that bubbles up
within him. In those long ago days when we saw much of each

The Mount, Cookham Dene, where Kenneth Grahame lived as a child from 1864 to 1866.

other, I always felt that, with all the frankness and jollity of his boyishness, there was also the boy's reticence and half-unconscious withdrawal into himself; and then again, beyond the boy, was a man known by few, remote, but very much to be reckoned with.''

And Robertson also added: ''Animals loved him. They felt safe with him, and indeed his presence ever brought a sense of security, like the shelter of a hill or the shadow of a great tree. His quiet strength soothed and sustained.''

This, then, was the man cooped up in the Bank of England who found expression through essays and stories for his interests in children and nature. But it would be wrong to think he found composition easy, which perhaps also explains the paucity of his output. He discussed this with Clayton Hamilton, an admiring Professor of English Literature from America, who visited him in 1923:

''A sentence that is easy to read may have been difficult to put together,'' he said. ''Perhaps the greater the easiness in writing, the harder that task in composition. Writing is not easy: I need not tell you that. There is always a pleasure in that exercise; but, also, there is always an agony in the endeavour. If we make a formula of those two motives, I think we may define the process. It is, at its best, a pleasurable agony.

''I am not a professional writer. I never have been, and I never will be, by reason of the accident that I don't need any money. I do not care for the notoriety: in fact, it is distasteful to me. If I should ever become a popular author, my privacy would be disrupted and I should no longer be allowed to live alone.

''What, then, is the use of writing for a person like myself? The answer might seem cryptic to most. It is merely that a fellow entertains a sort of hope that somehow, sometime, he may build a noble sentence that might make Sir Thomas Browne sit upward once again in that inhospitable grave of his in Norwich.''

Self-deprecating though Kenneth Grahame was about his work right up to the end of his life, he had already written that ''noble sentence'' – indeed a great many of them – long before this conversation took place. *The Wind in the Willows* was by then

already widely acknowledged as the masterpiece it undeniably is.
How he had come to create the book during his last years at the
Bank of England is well worth the telling.

Grahame had married Elspeth Thomson, the daughter of a
Scottish inventor, in July 1899, and in May 1900 they had their
only child, a son, Alastair. The boy was born prematurely and
suffered poor health for much of his short life. (He was killed on a
railway line at Oxford in May 1920.) During the child's infancy
he was doted on by both his parents who nick-named him
''Mouse''. He apparently became fascinated with books while he
was still very young, and one of Kenneth Grahame's favourite
chores was reading the boy a bed-time story as soon as he
returned from the Bank.

In his biography of Grahame, Patrick R. Chalmers tells us that
each night before dinner the father would slip into his small son's
nursery to read him something. ''For a while the nursery classics
served their purpose,'' Chalmers says. ''But when Alastair was a
four-year-old the classics were becoming exhausted.

''One May evening in 1904 the lady of the house, anxious that
she and her husband should not be *too* late in arriving at
Lancaster Gate and the dinner engagement which even now
awaited them, said rather impatiently to her maid, attentive in the
hall with cloak and fan and gloves, 'Where *is* Mr. Grahame,
Louise?'

''Louise, a Wiltshire woman who still, even in the shadow of
the Albert Memorial, used the archaic idiom of the Downs,
replied with a sniff, 'He's with Master Mouse, Madam; he's telling him some ditty or other about a Toad.'

''Now 'ditty', when used by a Downswoman, signifies, not
Song but Story. And so was *The Wind in the Willows* born and
Louise was its herald.''

The story actually developed slowly over the next four years, as
Grahame recounted incident after incident for his young listener.
It did not take anything like its final shape until the summer of
1907 when Mouse was holidaying apart from his parents at
Littlehampton. On May 10, Kenneth Grahame wrote a letter of
birthday wishes to his son, and as a postscript wrote a short

episode about the character Toad whom he had first introduced in the nursery. In fifteen succeeding letters he continued the adventures of the irrepressible Toad, and when these letters in their beautiful handwriting were carefully saved by the governess and returned to Kenneth Grahame at the end of the holiday, he had the raw material for his famous story.

Strange as it may seem today, when *The Wind in the Willows* was published it did not prove the immediate best-seller it should have been. Both publishers and later the public, conditioned by the success of *The Golden Age* and *Dream Days* to expect more of the same, were taken aback by this story written, not like the other – for adults about childhood – but for people of all ages, describing a world in which animals spoke and acted like human beings. A number of publishers had even rejected the manuscript before it was finally accepted by Messrs Methuen, and on publication in October 1908, several months of shocked silence and halting sales followed before the book embarked on its triumphant career of runaway success. *The Times* probably best summed up the general feeling of confusion over the story when its anonymous reviewer wrote, "Grown-up readers will find it monstrous and elusive, children will hope, in vain, for more fun. Beneath the allegory ordinary life is depicted more or less closely, but certainly not very amusingly or searchingly. As a contribution to natural history the work is negligible. For ourselves, we lay *The Wind in the Willows* reverently aside and again, for the hundredth time, take up *The Golden Age*."

Two men may perhaps be given the credit for tipping the balance of public opinion: the writer A. A. Milne (not yet the author of his string of children's classics featuring Christopher Robin and Winnie-the-Pooh which appeared in the nineteen-twenties), and none other than President Theodore Roosevelt of the United States, whose appreciative letter to the author, written in January 1909, described his gradual seduction by the characters of Mole, Rat, Badger and Toad.

"My dear Mr. Grahame," Roosevelt wrote from The White House on January 17, "My mind moves in ruts, as I suppose most minds do, and at first I could not reconcile myself to the change from the ever-delightful Harold and his associates, and so for some time I could not accept the toad, the mole, the water-rat and the badger as substitutes. But after a while Mrs. Roosevelt and two of the boys, Kermit and Ted, all quite independently, got hold of *The Wind Among the Willows* and took such a delight in it that I began to feel that I might have to revise my judgment. Then Mrs. Roosevelt read it aloud to the younger children, and I listened now and then. Now I have read it and reread it, and have come to accept the characters as old friends; and I am almost more fond of it than of your previous books. Indeed, I feel about going to Africa very much as the sea-faring rat did when he almost made the water-rat wish to forsake everything and start wandering!

''I felt I must give myself the pleasure of telling you how much we had all enjoyed your book.''

A. A. Milne, for his part, took his ardent campaign on behalf of the book into the popular press. In a later introduction to an edition of *The Wind in the Willows* published in 1940, he wrote, ''For years I have been talking about this book, quoting it, recommending it. In one of my early panegyrics I said: 'I feel sometimes that it was I who wrote it and recommended it to Kenneth Grahame.' '' And he added further on, ''One can argue over the merits of most books, and in arguing understand the point of view of one's opponent. One may even come to the conclusion that possibly he is right after all. One does not argue about *The Wind in the Willows*. The young man gives it to the girl with whom he is in love, and if she does not like it, asks her to return his letters. The older man tries it on his nephew, and alters his will accordingly. The book is a test of character. We can't criticise it, because it is criticising us. As I wrote once: It is a Household Book; a book which everybody in the household loves, and quotes continually; a book which is read aloud to every new guest and is regarded as the touchstone of his worth.''

Milne, of course, reaped his reward for his campaigning when he was invited to turn the book into a play. Despite his reservations, he produced *Toad of Toad Hall* which has proved a perennial Christmas favourite to this day.

Because of his declining health, Kenneth Grahame had, in fact, retired from the Bank of England on a modest pension before *The Wind in the Willows* became a success. But if he had any qualms about his finances in the years to come, these were quickly dispelled when royalties poured in from edition after edition – not only in Britain, but America and much of the rest of the world, too. These sales proved what a success the book now was with the public, and when reviewers again took up their copies and read more carefully and objectively what Grahame had written – freeing themselves from the prejudices of the earlier works – they unreservedly revised their opinions: thereafter placing Kenneth Grahame among the immortals of modern literature. He himself might not have been prepared to agree to such a thing, but one could almost sense Sir Thomas Browne sitting upright in his coffin!

Patrick Chalmers tells us that the original title for the book was to have been *The Wind in the Reeds*, but the publishers changed this because of the similarity to a collection of W. B. Yeats' poems, *The Wind Among The Reeds*. Grahame himself offered a second choice, *Mr. Mole and His Mates*, while his friend Graham Robertson proposed *The Lapping of the Stream, The Whispering Reeds, River Folk* or *The Children of Pan*.

To announce the book, Grahame was asked to provide a blurb for the publisher's catalogue, and his description makes fascinating reading. ''It is a book of Youth,'' he wrote, ''and so perhaps chiefly *for* Youth, and those who still keep the spirit of youth alive in them: of life, sunshine, running water, woodlands, dusty roads, winter firesides; free of problems, clear of the clash of sex; of life as it might fairly be supposed to be regarded by some of the wise small things, 'That glide in grasses and rubble of woody wreck.' ''

In compiling this work to mark the fiftieth anniversary of Kenneth Grahame's death, I have kept these fine ideals at the forefront of my mind.

Like all great works of literature, it would be wrong to think that *The Wind in the Willows* sprang fully-formed into its

creator's mind. As I have already mentioned, the episodes concerning Toad's adventures took shape in the oral stories and in
the letters which Grahame wrote to his son, Alastair. But as the
very title itself seems almost to suggest, elements of the book –
breezes if you like – had been blowing around in his mind for
many years. To illustrate what I mean, let me quote Grahame's
own words on the themes of a writer, given in a lecture at
Oxford.

"Remember," he said, "that a theme, a thesis, a subject, is in
most cases little more than a sort of clothes-line on which one
pegs a string of ideas, quotations, allusions, and so on, one's
mental under-garments of all shapes and sizes, some possibly
fairly new, but most rather old and patched; they dance and sway
in the breeze, they flap and flutter, or hang limp and lifeless. And
some are ordinary enough, and some are of a rather private and
intimate shape and give the owner away, even show up his or her
peculiarities. And, owing to the invisible clothes-line, they seem
to have connexion and continuity. And when they are
thoroughly aired, they are taken down and put away, and the
clothes-line is coiled up and disappears.

"Now talking of clothes-lines, I am reminded that Samuel
Butler was in the habit, during his walks abroad, of looking out
for any subjects that would do for plots for short stories. He never
wrote the short stories, but he collected the plots all the same.
Well, on one of his walks he saw a family wash hung out to dry.
The wind was strong, and the various garments, big and little,
were all behaving in the manner I have indicated, tossing, and
talking to each other apparently, and he thought what a good idea
for a love story. First you would have the various under-garments
of two families hung out to dry in adjacent gardens. A nightshirt
of one family would be observed, the wind being high, paying
more than particular attention to a lady's nightgown in another
garden. And the nightgown would be seen to reciprocate the
advances of the nightshirt. In due course both would be observed
hanging in a third garden by themselves. By and by, after a decent
interval of time of course, there would also be seen on that line – a
little night garment.

"This is meant by me as a parable, which is that ideas, illustrations, suggestions, my mental under-garments so to speak, have been swaying and fluttering before you while I speak. My only hope is that some garment on my clothes-line may stimulate some train of thought hanging on the clothes-line in your adjacent garden, and that the result may be, some day, a little mental nightshirt, or at least the tiniest of chemises."

It was, in fact, from Grahame's own wanderings abroad, first as a child, then as a form of escape from the demands of his life at the Bank of England, that he formed his own "clothes-line" and on it hung the "garments" of his experiences which in the fullness of time were to emerge as his "little mental nightshirt", *The Wind in the Willows*.

My view of the importance of this statement is also shared by another biographer, Eleanor Graham, who says that Grahame's idea of the "clothes-line" is a useful and thoroughly practical one. "He used it," she has said, "to show how a very odd collection of ideas and impressions, when brought together in the framework of a particular theme, yield, and melt, and become fused into something new. Looked at from another angle, his 'clothes-line' may become the drawstring on which are hung, in the same way, those rags and tatters which are the elements of a story."

Eleanor Graham believes he devised his "clothes-line" idea while composing the essays which formed the first of his collection, *Pagan Papers* (some of which are reprinted here), but once he had the invisible connection which bound all the ideas together, he was ready to create his masterpiece. "Of all that fluttered on the line when *The Wind in the Willows* was coming into being," she adds, "no more need be said."

Here, however, my view differs from that of Miss Graham. I believe that the "garments" which he used are valuable and revealing, enhancing our enjoyment and insight into that great novel. Hence this volume.

The very first elements are to be found during Kenneth Grahame's childhood, when he evidenced a love of nature and a profound desire to understand its creatures. He spent the years between the ages of four and seven at the home of his maternal grandmother, "Granny Ingles," following the premature death of his mother. Her house was called The Mount, a rambling old mansion surrounded by gardens, meadows and woods, which stood at Cookham Dene on the banks of the River Thames. Here his wandering footsteps and lively imagination took him into the world of nature which he was never really to leave. There were molehills to observe, badgers to follow, and toads to watch among the rushes and long grass. Along the river bank which he explored were the homes of water rats, and beyond the bends in the river, the open countryside which was to weave such a spell over him when the coming of age gave him the freedom to come and go as he liked.

"In those few rich years," says Eleanor Graham, "lay the seeds of *The Golden Age*, and much of the inspiration which went to make the perfection of *The Wind in the Willows*, since he carried in him for the rest of his life exact and brilliant memories of what it had felt like to be a boy of four, of five, of six, of seven." (Aside from the stories which Grahame wrote based on his childhood and which appeared in *The Golden Age* and *Dream Days*, he also wrote a fascinating and little known essay about this period of his life and his feelings which appeared in the *New Review* of March 1896. As "Secret Kingdoms" has never been published in a book collection before and also reveals what are, in effect, the beginnings of Kenneth Grahame's three great books, I have reprinted it as an Appendix to this volume.)

Such was the impression that these days among nature had on young Kenneth that it is no surprise to find that when he grew older he was inexorably drawn back to the same vicinity, or that when the urge came upon him to write he should put some of this continuing fascination into words. In these early essays are to be found many of the elements that later appeared in *The Wind in the Willows*, perhaps stated very simply and sometimes with less clarity, but there none the less; and when he began work on his tale of the river bank and its inhabitants he borrowed freely and unashamedly from these "pathways" – sometimes taking little more than a single idea for any one chapter, while in others

embracing the whole concept of the original essay. As another of
Grahame's biographers, Peter Green, has observed:

"The main motifs behind *The Wind in the Willows* [are] their
personal and historical impulses in Grahame's mind. There is the
idealised river landscape with its peaceful Epicurean inhabitants;
the menace, finally destroyed, of the Wild Wood; the conflict
between a paternalistic society and the hubristic, Bohemian
individual, as exemplified by Toad; and the stabilisation of the
traditional *status quo* by the realisation of a completely self-
contained and self-sufficient myth . . . this myth was constructed
from diverse elements in Grahame's life and background, and en-
riched by constant associative allusions.''

We should not forget that Grahame had literary influences,
too. As a small child he loved *Aesop 's Fables*, and in 1899 he
wrote an introduction to a new edition of this work, incorporating
several elements which later found their way into "The Wild
Wood" chapter of his novel. In 1881, the year it was published
in Britain, Kenneth discovered *Uncle Remus* by Joel Chandler
Harris (1848–1908), and thereafter – according to a relative –
"he was continually reading and quoting from it." This work,
mixing folklore and the world of animals, remained a favourite
throughout his life. Thirdly, he was a great admirer of the work of
the now almost forgotten American, Eugene Field (1850–95), a
humorist and versifier who wrote a number of children's poems,
including the popular nursery lullaby, "Wynken, Blynken and
Nod". Grahame discovered his world of "nonsense" while still
very young, and cherished the memory of Field strongly enough
to be persuaded to write a preface to a posthumous collection of
his work published in 1898. This delightful short essay, now of
considerable rarity, is also included in the Appendix to this
book.

Essentially, though, as I have made evident, Kenneth
Grahame's main influences were the River Thames and the
surrounding countryside of Berkshire and Oxfordshire. And in
the pages which follow I have set out to show how carefully and
lovingly he had explored some of the paths which led to the river
bank and thence along the open roads of the English countryside,

*Kenneth Grahame – a sketch made at the Bank of
England during the 1890s.*

before he so magically evoked them in the pages of his tale of Mole, Rat, Badger and Toad. (It is interesting to note, incidentally, that years after *The Wind in the Willows* was published, Grahame was pressed by a correspondent to say on which side of the Thames the famous river bank was based. Carefully he replied that he thought there was ''just as much of Oxfordshire as Berkshire in it,'' and he went on: ''Some of the animals must have lived on one side of the river, and some on the other; but I have always felt sure that Toad Hall was on the Oxfordshire side.'')

A few of these essays and reflections on the countryside which so absorbed him were reprinted in the volume *Pagan Papers*, a work now long out of print and practically unobtainable. Others – the majority – Grahame confined to the pages of the magazines and journals to which they were contributed, and they have never since graced the printed page. As he considered them work he had written while he was striving to find his authentic ''voice'', he saw no point in their reappearance during his life time. Whether he suppressed them as evidence of the creative process that gave birth to *The Wind in the Willows* is debatable, but as a man who carefully supervised the publication of all his work, it is arguable that he wished his novel to be assessed purely on its own merits, without recourse to outside influences – a favourite pastime, he knew, of certain critics and intellectuals. As a book which has remained a favourite with generation after generation and continues to grow in esteem, it now seems a perfectly legitimate exercise to rescue these important essays from the obscurity that has hidden them – in most cases for nearly a century – and by rereading them to see how they formed pathways to *The Wind in the Willows*.

The pieces beautifully evoke the lovely countryside of Berkshire, Oxfordshire and the Thames Valley where Grahame lived for much of his life, and where he quite naturally chose to locate his novel. They are also revealing of their author's concern for the environment (Grahame was nothing if not a pioneer conservationist), his enjoyment of wandering on foot, and his yearning for places just beyond the horizon. Although he is forever associated with this part of England, Kenneth Grahame also loved Cornwall where he frequently holidayed (absorbing some of its beauties into *The Wind in the Willows*) and until the last day of his life often pined after the sun and the warmth to be found in southern climes.

Readers who are familiar with *The Wind in the Willows* – and they will be legion for it is not a book read once, but returned to again and again – will probably have no difficulty in appreciating the similarities between Kenneth Grahame's essays in this collection and the chapters they foreshadowed in his story. They are, however, arranged wherever possible in the same order as the twelve chapters in *The Wind in the Willows*, and each is prefaced by what I trust will prove interesting and revealing details about their contents and original place of publication. Taken both individually and collectively, I think they can only enhance our interest in Grahame's masterpiece, and underline still more emphatically what a wonderful chronicler of the countryside he was. Time, thankfully, has not changed too much of the scenery that he described, and I hope that the evocative sketches by Carolyn Beresford which accompany the text will encourage the reader to visit this beautiful area.

Above all, however, I hope that the reader will enjoy the essays for their own intrinsic worth. Kenneth Grahame was a master of English prose, his impressions and opinions expressed with crystalline clearness, his phrases turned with precision and deftness. Enjoy them, then, as you might those stories which Rat told poor Mole after he had rescued him from the river and made him comfortable in his home before a bright fire:

"Very thrilling stories they were, too, to an earth-dwelling animal like Mole. Stories about weirs, and sudden floods, and leaping pike, and steamers that flung hard bottles – at least bottles were certainly flung, and *from* steamers, so presumably *by* them; and about herons, and how particular they were whom they spoke to; and about adventures down drains, and night-fishings with Otter; or excursions far afield with Badger."

Like Mole, Rat, Badger, Mr. Toad and all their friends, I believe you will find in these pages "something of what goes whispering so constantly among the reed-stems'' and of which Kenneth Grahame was a writer without peer.

PETER HAINING
Boxford, Suffolk.
October, 1982.

1

"Riverside Life"

"Kenneth Grahame," says one of his biographers, Eleanor Graham, "was drawing on actual memories for many of his descriptions in *The Wind in the Willows* and they catch in the mind till they have the feeling of personal experiences."

This is a statement that becomes self-evident from the first pages of the story, and it is in no way surprising to learn that Mole's sudden urge to flee from his tiresome chores and take himself into the warm, spring day beyond the confines of his little home, was something Grahame had pined after ever since his own incarceration within the gloomy portals of the Bank of England in London. Nor should we be surprised to find that this longing was vividly expressed in one of his earliest published essays, "The Rural Pan", which appeared in the *National Observer* of April 25, 1891. It was one of his first contributions to that magazine and with it, Patrick Chalmers says, "he had turned up trumps, and his literary future was, if he so wished, made."

Long before, during his childhood at Cookham Dene, Grahame had discovered the joys of boating or wandering along the banks of the River Thames on lazy, sunlit days. As he sat at his desk in Threadneedle Street with the sun outside reminding him of just such times, his impatience for the weekend when he could once again return was precisely the same motivation with which he later endowed Mole. He took both the feeling and atmosphere of "The Rural Pan" in creating the opening of his novel, even to the introduction of a water rat. Who would deny that he is the prototype of the kindly Water Rat of *The Wind in the Willows*?

(There are also foretastes here of the river journey made by Mole and Rat in the chapter "The Piper at the Gates of Dawn", while the central figure in that section of the book is, of course, Pan.)

The dreamy, lyrical day which Mole and Rat spend on the river, pausing to picnic and to allow Mole his ill-fated attempt at rowing, are like many that Grahame himself enjoyed: not just on the Thames but casually roaming the surrounding countryside. Again, the forerunner of these pages is to be found in an early essay perfectly entitled, "Loafing", also written for the *National Observer*, and published slightly earlier, in January 1891. Biographer Peter Green writes, "The core of reality, in this case, is that stretch of the Thames which runs, roughly, from Marlow to Pangbourne; and in particular the area around Cookham Dene. This had the most powerful and emotive associations for him. He had known it during his most impressionable period as a child; he had returned to it in middle age, drawn by the compulsive and no longer to be neglected memories. Here he had spent – and still spent – long hours in backwater or eyot, watching water rats, moles, otters, and toads go about their private business. This was the still centre upon which the book evolved." Emphasising still further the importance of the two essays which follow here, Mr. Green adds, "This idealisation of the River Bank had very deep roots in Grahame's past."

These, then, are the accounts of weekends spent round and about the Thames, from which "The River Bank" grew. And it should be remembered, too, that it was at Cookham Dene in 1907 that Kenneth Grahame finally committed to paper the whole adventures of the River Bankers from the first emergence of Mole into the sunlight to the very last "base libel on Badger".

* * *

THE RURAL PAN

THROUGH shady Throgmorton Street and about the vale of Cheapside the restless Mercury is flitting, with furtive eye and voice a little hoarse from bidding in the market. Further

The Thames near Pangbourne, the stretch of river that inspired the setting for The Wind in the Willows.

west, down classic Piccadilly, moves the young Apollo, the lord of the unerring (satin) bow; and nothing meaner than a frockcoat shall in these latter years float round his perfect limbs. But remote in other haunts than these the rural Pan is hiding, and piping the low, sweet strain that reaches only the ears of a chosen few. And now that the year wearily turns and stretches herself before the perfect waking, the god emboldened begins to blow a clearer note.

When the waking comes at last, and Summer is abroad, these deities will abroad too, each as his several attributes move him. Who is this that flieth up the reaches of the Thames in steam-launch hired for the day? Mercury is out – some dozen or fifteen strong. The flower-gemmed banks crumble and slide down under the wash of his rampant screw; his wake is marked by a line of lobster-claws, gold-necked bottles, and fragments of veal-pie. Resplendent in blazer, he may even be seen to embrace the slim-waisted nymph, haunter of green (room) shades, in the full gaze of the shocked and scandalised sun. Apollo meantime reposeth, passively beautiful, on the lawn of the Guards' Club at Maidenhead. Here, O Apollo, are haunts meet for thee. A deity subjectively inclined, he is neither objective nor, it must be said for him, at all objectionable, like them of Mercury.

Meanwhile, nor launches nor lawns tempt him that pursueth the rural Pan. In the hushed recesses of Hurley backwater, where the canoe may be paddled almost under the tumbling comb of the weir, he is to be looked for; there the god pipes with freest abandonment. Or under the great shadow of Streatley Hill, "annihilating all that's made to a green thought in a green shade"; or better yet, pushing an explorer's prow up the remote untravelled Thame, till Dorchester's stately roof broods over the quiet fields. In solitudes such as these Pan sits and dabbles, and all the air is full of the music of his piping. Southwards, again, on the pleasant Surrey downs there is shouting and jostling; dust that is drouthy and language that is sultry. Thither comes the young Apollo, calmly confident as ever; and he meeteth certain Mercuries of the baser sort, who do him obeisance, call him captain and lord, and then proceed to skin him from head to foot as thoroughly as the god himself flayed Marsyas in days of yore, at a certain Spring Meeting in Phrygia: a good instance of Time's revenges. And yet Apollo returns to town and swears he has had a grand day. He does so every year. Out of hearing of all the clamour, the rural Pan may be found stretched on Ranmore Common, loitering under Abinger pines, or prone by the secluded stream of the sinuous Mole, abounding in friendly greetings for his foster-brothers the dab-chick and water-rat.

For a holiday, Mercury loveth the Pullman Express, and a short hour with a society paper; anon, brown boots on the pier, and the pleasant combination of Métropole and Monopole. Apollo for his part will urge the horses of the Sun: and, if he leaveth the society weekly to Mercury, yet he loveth well the Magazine. From which ὀμφαλός or hub of the universe he will direct his shining team even to the far Hesperides of Richmond or of Windsor. Both iron road and level highway are shunned by the rural Pan, who chooses rather to foot it along the sheep track on the limitless downs or the thwart-leading footpath through copse and spinney, not without pleasant fellowship with feather and fur. Nor does it follow from all this that the god is unsocial. Albeit shy of the company of his more showy brother-deities, he loveth the more unpretentious humankind, especially them that are *adscripti glebæ*, addicted to the kindly soil and to the working thereof: perfect in no way, only simple, cheery sinners. For he is only half a god after all, and the red earth in him is strong. When the pelting storm drives the wayfarers to the sheltering inn, among the little group on bench and settle Pan has been known to appear at times, in homely guise of hedger-and-ditcher or weather-beaten shepherd from the downs. Strange lore and quaint fancy he will then impart, in the musical Wessex or Mercian he has learned to speak so naturally; though it may not be till many a mile away that you begin to suspect that you have unwittingly talked with him who chased the flying Syrinx in Arcady and turned the tide of fight at Marathon.

Yes: today the iron horse has searched the country through – east and west, north and south – bringing with it Commercialism, whose god is Jerry, and who studs the hills with stucco and garrotes the streams with the girder. Bringing, too, into every

nook and corner fashion and chatter, the tailor-made gown and
the eyeglass. Happily a great part is still spared – how great these
others fortunately do not know – in which the rural Pan and his
following may hide their heads for yet a little longer, until the
growing tyranny has invaded the last common, spinney, and
sheep-down, and driven the kindly god, the well-wisher to man –
whither?

*   *   *

LOAFING

WHEN the golden Summer has rounded languidly to his
close, when Autumn has been carried forth in russet
winding-sheet, then all good fellows who look upon holidays as a
chief end of life return from moor and stream and begin to take
stock of gains and losses. And the wisest, realising that the time
of action is over while that of reminiscence has begun, realise too
that the one is pregnant with greater pleasures than the other –
that action, indeed, is only the means to an end of reflection and
appreciation. Wisest of all, the Loafer stands apart supreme. For
he, of one mind with the philosopher as to the end, goes straight
to it at once, and his happy summer has accordingly been spent in
those subjective pleasures of the mind whereof the others, the
men of muscle and peeled faces, are only just beginning to taste.

And yet though he may a little despise (or rather pity) them,
the Loafer does not dislike nor altogether shun them. Far from it:
they are very necessary to him. For "*Suave mari magno*" is the
motto of your true Loafer; and it is chiefly by keeping ever in view
the struggles and the clamorous jostlings of the unenlightened
making holiday that he is able to realise the bliss of his own
condition and maintain his self-satisfaction at boiling-point. And
so is he never very far away from the track beaten by the hurrying
Philistine hoof, but hovers more or less on the edge of it,
where, the sole fixed star amidst whirling constellations, he may
watch the mad world "glance, and nod, and hurry by."

There are many such centres of contemplation along the West

Coast of Scotland. Few places are better loafing-ground than a pier, with its tranquil "lucid interval" between steamers, the ever recurrent throb of paddle-wheel, the rush and foam of beaten water among the piles, splash of ropes and rumble of gangways, and all the attendant hurry and scurry of the human morrice. Here, *tanquam in speculo*, the Loafer as he lounges may, by attorney as it were, touch gently every stop in the great organ of the emotions of mortality. Rapture of meeting, departing woe, love at first sight, disdain, laughter, indifference – he may experience them all, but attenuated and as if he saw them in a dream; as if, indeed, he were Heine's god in dream on a mountain-side. Let the drowsy deity awake, and all these puppets, emanations of his dream, will vanish into the nothing whence they came. And these emotions may be renewed each morning; if a fair one sail today, be sure that one as fair will land tomorrow. The supply is inexhaustible.

But in the South perhaps the happiest loafing-ground is the gift of Father Thames; for there again the contrast of violent action, with its blisters, perspiration, and the like, throws into fine relief the bliss of "quietism." I know one little village in the upper reaches where loafing may be pushed to high perfection. Here the early hours of the morning are vexed by the voice of boaters making their way down the little street to the river. The most of them go staggering under hampers, bundles of waterproofs, and so forth. Their voices are clamant of feats to be accomplished: they will row, they will punt, they will paddle, till they weary out the sun. All this the Loafer hears through the open door of his cottage, where in his shirt-sleeves he is dallying with his bacon, as a gentleman should. He is the only one who has had a comfortable breakfast – and he knows it. Later he will issue forth and stroll down in their track to the bridge. The last of these Argonauts is pulling lustily forth; the river is dotted with evanishing blazers. Upon all these lunatics a pitiless Phœbus shines triumphant. The Loafer sees the last of them off the stage, turns his back on it, and seeks the shady side of the street.

A holy calm possesses the village now; the foreign element has passed away with shouting and waving of banners, and its natural

life of somnolency is in evidence at last. And first, as a true Loafer
should, let him respectfully greet each several village dog.
Arcades ambo – loafers likewise – they lie there in the warm dust,
each outside his own door, ready to return the smallest courtesy.
Their own lords and masters are not given to the exchange of
compliments nor to greetings in the market-place. The dog is
generally the better gentleman, and he is aware of it; and he duly
appreciates the Loafer, who is not too proud to pause a moment,
change the news, and pass the time of day. He will mark his sense
of this attention by rising from his dust-divan and accompanying
his caller some steps on his way. But he will stop short of his
neighbour's dust-patch; for the morning is really too hot for a
shindy. So, by easy stages (the street is not a long one: six dogs
will see it out), the Loafer quits the village; and now the world is
before him. Shall he sit on a gate and smoke? or lie on the grass
and smoke? or smoke aimlessly and at large along the road? Such
a choice of happiness is distracting; but perhaps the last course is
the best – as needing the least mental effort of selection. Hardly,
however, has he fairly started his first day-dream when the
snappish ''ting'' of a bellkin recalls him to realities. By comes the
bicyclist: dusty, sweating, a piteous thing to look upon. But the
irritation of the strepitant metal has jarred the Loafer's always
exquisite nerves: he is fain to climb a gate and make his way
towards solitude and the breezy downs.

Up here all vestiges of a sordid humanity disappear. The
Loafer is alone with the south-west wind and the blue sky. Only
a carolling of larks and a tinkling from distant flocks break
the brooding noonday stillness; above, the wind-hover hangs
motionless, a black dot on the blue. Prone on his back on the
springy turf, gazing up into the sky, his fleshy integument seems
to drop away, and the spirit ranges at will among the tranquil
clouds. This way Nirvana nearest lies. Earth no longer obtrudes
herself; possibly somewhere a thousand miles or so below him the
thing still ''spins like a fretful midge.'' The Loafer knows not nor
cares. His is now an astral body, and through golden spaces of
imagination his soul is winging her untrammelled flight. And
there he really might remain for ever, but that his vagrom spirit is

called back to earth by a gentle but resistless, very human summons, – a gradual, consuming, Pantagruelian, god-like, thirst: a thirst to thank Heaven on. So, with a sigh half of regret, half of anticipation, he bends his solitary steps towards the nearest inn. Tobacco for one is good; to commune with oneself and be still is truest wisdom; but beer is a thing of deity – beer is divine.

Later the Loafer may decently make some concession to popular taste by strolling down to the river and getting out his boat. With one paddle out he will drift down the stream: just brushing the flowering rush and the meadow-sweet and taking in as peculiar gifts the varied sweets of even. The loosestrife is his, and the arrow-head: his the distant moan of the weir; his are the glories, amber and scarlet and silver, of the sunset-haunted surface. By-and-by the boaters will pass him homeward-bound. All are blistered and sore: his withers are unwrung. Most are too tired and hungry to see the sunset glories; no corporeal pangs clog his *æsthesis* – his perceptive faculty. Some have quarrelled in the day and are no longer on speaking terms; he is at peace with himself and with the whole world. Of all that lay them down in the little village that night, his sleep will be the surest and the sweetest. For not even the blacksmith himself will have better claim to have earned a night's repose.

2

"On the High Road"

It was not only the stretches of green and verdant pastures alongside the River Thames that captivated Kenneth Grahame's heart and soul. He also fell under the spell of the Berkshire Downs rising majestically away on the horizon, and on hot summer days the open roads which lay beneath him, like inviting paths to untold joys, rarely failed to draw his restless feet.

Grahame's love of wandering across this beautiful landscape, sometimes into Berkshire and occasionally in the other direction over the high ground of Oxfordshire, was early born and never left him, even in old age. He felt in his bones the urge to take to the high road, and his characters in *The Wind in the Willows*, in particular Toad, all share this feeling to a greater or lesser degree.

Our first introduction to the owner of Toad Hall in the second chapter of the book, "The Open Road", finds him poring over a map and dreaming of distant horizons. Tired of boating on the river, he has bought himself a gypsy caravan painted canary yellow. He is soon enthusing about it to Mole and Rat:

"There's real life for you, embodied in that little cart," he declares, indicating his new pride and joy. "The open road, the dusty highway, the heath, the common, the hedgerows, the rolling downs! Camps, villages, towns, cities! Here today, up and off to somewhere else tomorrow! Travel, change, interest, excitement! The whole world before you, and a horizon that's always changing!"

These are words I can imagine Kenneth Grahame himself saying, indeed he may well have done so. What is beyond dispute is that very similar words were spoken to him by a former clerk at

*The Ridgeway, the ancient trackway running along the
top of the Berkshire Downs where Grahame loved to
wander.*

the Bank of England who, fired by the same impulses, bought
himself a little cart and was thereafter "lost to the world of
London". That Toad has something of Fothergill in him may be
further gleaned from the fact that the banker had a large house
and servants and possessed a total indifference to money.

Of course, there is part of Grahame in Toad, too, but he did not
take to the high roads in a cart in quite the same way as Fothergill,
although how much the idea appealed to him is clearly indicated in
"A Bohemian in Exile" which he wrote for the *St. James'
Gazette* of September 27, 1890. Peter Green has said of this essay

that it "provides a link between the repressed Bohemian of his earlier work and Toad's curious behaviour in *The Wind in the Willows*." What we learn of Fothergill's motivations, and his adventures across the North Berkshire Downs in particular, are duplicated to an extraordinary degree in the wanderings of the three little friends in their yellow gypsy caravan.

During the course of their journey along "The Open Road", Mole, Rat and Toad "ramble over grassy downs" and then take to "strolling along the high road", both descriptions reminiscent of the beautiful stretch of high ground in North Berkshire known as the Ridgeway. This ancient trackway had long been a favourite haunt of Kenneth Grahame, as several of his friends have told us, and as he himself confessed in another early essay, most appropriately called "The Romance of the Road". This was a contribution to the *National Observer* of February 14, 1891, and in it the reader will discover the same love of this part of the countryside which is so apparent in "The Open Road" – indeed, all that is missing is the motor car which ruins the rural calm, yet bewitches the impressionable Toad and inadvertently sets him off on the series of foolhardy adventures that run through the rest of the book.

* * *

A BOHEMIAN IN EXILE

WHEN, many years ago now, the once potent and extensive kingdom of Bohemia gradually dissolved and passed away, not a few historians were found to chronicle its past glories; and some have gone on to tell the fate of this or that once powerful chieftain who either donned the swallow-tail and conformed or, proudly self-exiled, sought some quiet retreat and died as he had lived, a Bohemian. But these were of the princes of the land. To the people, the villeins, the common rank and file, does no interest attach? Did they waste and pine, anaemic, in thin, strange, unwonted air? Or sit at the table of the scornful and learn, with Dante, how salt was alien bread? It is of one of those faithful commons I would speak, narrating only "the short and simple annals of the poor."

It is to be noted that the kingdom aforesaid was not so much a kingdom as a United States – a collection of self-ruling guilds, municipalities, or republics, bound together by a common method of viewing life. "There *once* was a king of Bohemia" – but that was a long time ago, and even Corporal Trim was not certain in whose reign it was. These small free States, then, broke up gradually, from various causes and with varying speed; and I think ours was one of the last to go.

With us, as with many others, it was a case of lost leaders. "Just for a handful of silver he left us"; though it was not exactly that, but rather that, having got the handful of silver, they wanted a wider horizon to fling it about under than Bloomsbury afforded.

"So they left us for their pleasure; and in due time, one by one – "

But I will not be morose about them; they had honestly earned their success, and we all honestly rejoiced at it, and do so still.

When old Pan was dead and Apollo's bow broken, there were many faithful pagans who would worship at no new shrines, but went out to the hills and caves, truer to the old gods in their discrowned desolation than in their pomp and power. Even so were we left behind, a remnant of the faithful. We had never expected to become great in art or song; it was the life itself that we loved; that was our end – not, as with them, the means to an end.

"We aimed at no glory, no lovers of glory we;
Give us the glory of going on and still to be."

Unfortunately, going on was no longer possible; the old order had changed, and we could only patch up our broken lives as best might be.

Fothergill said that he, for one, would have no more of it. The past was dead, and he wasn't going to try to revive it. Henceforth he, too, would be dead to Bloomsbury. Our forefathers, speaking of a man's death, said "he changed his life". This is how

Fothergill changed his life and died to Bloomsbury. One morning
he made his way to the Whitechapel Road, and there he bought a
barrow. The Whitechapel barrows are of all sizes, from the
barrow wheeled about by a boy with half a dozen heads of
cabbages to barrows drawn by a tall pony, such as on Sundays
take the members of a club to Epping Forest. They are all
precisely the same in plan and construction, only in the larger
sizes the handles develop or evolve into shafts; and they are
equally suitable, according to size, for the vending of whelks, for a
hot-potato can, a piano organ, or for the conveyance of a cheery
and numerous party to the Derby. Forthergill bought a medium
sized ''developed'' one, and also a donkey to fit; he had it painted
white, picked out with green – the barrow, not the donkey – and
when his arrangements were complete, stabled the whole for
the night in Bloomsbury. The following morning, before the
early red had quite faded from the sky, the exodus took place,
those of us who were left being assembled to drink a parting
whisky-and-milk in sad and solemn silence. Forthergill turned
down Oxford Street, sitting on the shaft with a short clay in his
mouth, and disappeared from our sight, heading west at a
leisurely pace. So he passed out of our lives by way of the
Bayswater Road.

They must have wandered far and seen many things, he and
his donkey, from the fitful fragments of news that now and again
reached us. It seems that eventually, his style of living being
economical, he was enabled to put down his donkey and barrow,
and set up a cart and a mare – no fashionable gipsy-cart, a sort of
house-boat on wheels, but a light and serviceable cart, with a
moveable tilt, constructed on his own designs. This allowed him
to take along with him a few canvases and other artists' materials;
soda-water, whisky, and such like necessaries; and even to ask a
friend from town for a day or two, if he wanted to.

He was in this state of comparative luxury when at last, by the
merest accident, I foregathered with him once more. I had pulled
up to Streatley one afternoon, and, leaving my boat, had gone for
a long ramble on the glorious North Berkshire Downs to stretch
my legs before dinner. Somewhere over on Cuckhamsley Hill, by

the side of the Ridgeway, remote from the habitable world, I found him, smoking his vesper pipe on the shaft of his cart, the mare cropping the short grass beside him. He greeted me without surprise or effusion, as if we had only parted yesterday, and without a hint of an allusion to past times, but drifted quietly into rambling talk of his last three years, and, without ever telling his story right out, left a strange picturesque impression of a nomadic life which struck one as separated by fifty years from modern conventional existence. The old road-life still lingered on in places, it seemed, once one got well away from the railway: there were two Englands existing together, the one fringing the great iron highways wherever they might go – the England under the eyes of most of us. The other, unguessed at by many, in whatever places were still vacant of shriek and rattle, drowsed on as of old: the England of heath and common and windy sheep down, of by-lanes and village-greens – the England of Parson Adams and Lavengro. The spell of the free untrammelled life came over me as I listened, till I was fain to accept of his hospitality and a horse-blanket for the night, oblivious of civilised comforts down at the Bull. On the downs where Alfred fought we lay and smoked, gazing up at the quiet stars that had shone on many a Dane lying stark and still a thousand years ago; and in the silence of the lone tract that enfolded us we seemed nearer to those old times than to these I had left that afternoon, in the now hushed and sleeping valley of the Thames.

When the news reached me, some time later, that Fothergill's aunt had died and left him her house near town and the little all she had possessed, I heard it with misgivings, not to say forebodings. For the house had been his grandfather's, and he had spent much of his boyhood there; it had been a dream of his early days to possess it in some happy future, and I knew he could never bear to sell or let it. On the other hand, can you stall the wild ass of the desert? And will not the caged eagle mope and pine?

However, possession was entered into, and all seemed to go well for the time. The cart was honourably installed in the coach-house, the mare turned out to grass. Fothergill lived idly and happily, to all seeming, with "a book of verses underneath the bough", and a bottle of old claret for the friend who might chance to drop in. But as the year wore on small signs began to appear that he who had always "rather hear the lark sing than the mouse squeak" was beginning to feel himself caged, though his bars were gilded.

I was talking one day to his coachman (he now kept three men-servants), and he told me that of a Sunday morning when the household had gone to church and everything was quiet, Mr. Fothergill would go into the coach-house and light his pipe, and sit on the step of the brougham (he had a brougham now), and gaze at the old cart, and smoke and say nothing; and smoke and say nothing again. He didn't like it, the coachman confessed; and to me it seemed ominous.

One morning late in March, at the end of a long hard winter, I was wakened by a flood of sunshine. The early air came warm and soft through the open window; the first magic suggestion of spring was abroad, with its whispered hints of daffodils and budding hawthorns; and one's blood danced to imagined pipings of Pan from happy fields far distant. At once I thought of Fother-gill, and, with a certain foreboding of ill, made my way down to Holly Lodge as soon as possible. It was with no surprise at all that I heard that the master was missing. In the very first of the morn-ing, it seemed, or ever the earliest under-housemaid had begun to set man-traps on the stairs and along the passages, he must have quietly left the house. The servants were cheerful enough, never-theless, and thought the master must only have "gone for a nice long walk", and so on, after the manner of their kind. Without a word I turned my steps to the coach-house. Sure enough, the old cart was missing; the mare was gone from the paddock. It was no good my saying anything; pursuit of this wild haunter of tracks and by-paths would have been futile indeed. So I kept my own counsel. Fothergill never returned to Holly Lodge, and has been more secret and evasive since his last flight, rarely venturing on old camping grounds near home, like to a bird scared by the fowler's gun.

Once indeed, since then, while engaged in pursuit of the shy quarry known as the Early Perp., late Dec., E. Eng., and the like, specimens of which I was tracking down in the west, I hit upon him by accident; hearing in an old village rumours concerning a strange man in a cart who neither carried samples nor pushed the brewing interest by other means than average personal consumption – tales already beginning to be distorted into material for the myth of the future. I found him friendly as ever, equally ready to spin his yarns. As the evening wore on, I ventured upon an allusion to past times and Holly Lodge; but his air of puzzled politeness convinced me that the whole thing had passed out of his mind as a slight but disagreeable incident in the even tenor of his nomadic existence.

After all, his gains may have outbalanced his losses. Had he cared, he might, with his conversational gifts, have been a social success; certainly, I think, an artistic one. He had great powers, had any impulse been present to urge him to execution and achievement. But he was for none of these things. Contemplative, receptive, with a keen sense of certain sub-tones and side-aspects of life unseen by most, he doubtless chose wisely to enjoy life his own way, and to gather from the fleeting days what bliss they had to give, nor spend them in toiling for a harvest to be reaped when he was dust.

> Some for the glories of this life, and some
> Sigh for the Prophet's Paradise to come:
> Ah, take the cash and let the credit go,
> Nor heed the rumble of a distant drum.

* * *

THE ROMANCE OF THE ROAD

AMONG the many places of magic visited by Pantagruel and his company during the progress of their famous voyage, few surpass that island whose roads did literally "go" to places – "ou les chemins cheminent, comme animaulx": and would-be travellers, having inquired of the road as to its destination, and received satisfactory reply, "se guindans" (as the old book hath it – hoisting themselves up on) *''au chemin opportun, sans aultrement se poiner ou fatiguer, se trouvoyent au lieu destiné.''*

The best example I know of an approach to this excellent sort of vitality in roads is the Ridgeway of the North Berkshire Downs. Join it at Streatley, the point where it crosses the Thames; at once it strikes you out and away from the habitable world in a splendid, purposeful manner, running along the highest ridge of the Downs a broad green ribbon of turf, with but a shade of difference from the neighbouring grass, yet distinct for all that. No villages nor homesteads tempt it aside or modify its course for a yard; should you lose the track where it is blent with the bordering turf or merged in and obliterated by criss-cross paths, you have only to walk straight on, taking heed of no alternative to right or left; and in a minute 'tis with you again – arisen out of the earth as it were. Or, if still not quite assured, lift you your eyes, and there it runs over the brow of the fronting hill. Where a railway crosses it, it disappears indeed – hiding Alpheus-like, from the ignominy of rubble and brick-work; but a little way on it takes up the running again with the same quiet persistence. Out on that almost trackless expanse of billowy Downs such a track is in some sort humanly companionable: it really seems to lead you by the hand.

The ''Rudge'' is of course an exceptional instance; but indeed this pleasant personality in roads is not entirely fanciful. It exists as a characteristic of the old country road, evolved out of the primitive prehistoric track, developing according to the needs of the land it passes through and serves: with a language, accordingly, and a meaning of its own. Its special services are often told clearly enough; but much else too of the quiet story of the country-side: something of the old tale whereof you learn so little from the printed page. Each is instinct, perhaps, with a separate suggestion. Some are martial and historic, and by your side the hurrying feet of the dead raise a ghostly dust. The name of yon town – with its Roman or Saxon suffix to British root – hints at much. Many a strong man, wanting his *vates sacer*, passed silently to Hades for that suffix to obtain. The little rise up yonder on the Downs that breaks their straight green line against the sky showed another sight when the sea of battle surged and beat on its trampled sides; and the Roman, sore beset, may have gazed down this very road for relief, praying for night or the succouring legion. This child that swings on a gate and peeps at you from under her sun-bonnet – so may some girl-ancestress of hers have watched with beating heart the Wessex levies hurry along to clash with the heathen and break them on the down where the ash-trees grew. And yonder, where the road swings round under gloomy overgrowth of drooping boughs – is that gleam of water or glitter of lurking spears?

Some sing you pastorals, fluting low in the hot sun between dusty hedges overlooked by contented cows; past farmsteads where man and beast, living in frank fellowship, learn pleasant and serviceable lessons each of the other; over the full-fed river, lipping the meadow-sweet, and thence on either side through leagues of hay. Or through bending corn they chant the mystical wonderful song of the reaper when the harvest is white to the sickle. But most of them, avoiding classification, keep each his several tender significance: as with one I know, not so far from town, which woos you from the valley by gentle ascent between nut-laden hedges, and ever by some touch of keen fragrance in the air, by some mystery of added softness under foot – ever a promise of something to come, unguessed, delighting. Till suddenly you are among the pines, their keen scent strikes you through and through, their needles carpet the ground, and in their swaying tops moans the unappeasable wind – sad, ceaseless, as the cry of a warped humanity. Some paces more, and the promise is fulfilled, the hints and whisperings become fruition: the ground breaks steeply away, and you look over a great inland sea of fields, homesteads, rolling woodland, and – bounding all, blent with the horizon, a greyness, a gleam – the English Channel. A road of promises, of hinted surprises, following each other with the inevitable sequence in a melody.

But we are now in another and stricter sense an island of *chemins qui cheminent:* dominated, indeed, by them. By these the traveller, veritably *se guindans,* may reach his destination *"sans se poiner ou se fatiguer"* (with large qualifications); but *sans* very much else whereof he were none the worse. The gain seems so obvious that you forget to miss all that lay between the springing stride of the early start and the pleasant weariness of the end approached, when the limbs lag a little as the lights of your destination begin to glimmer through the dusk. All that lay between! "A Day's Ride a Life's Romance" was the excellent title of an unsuccessful book; and indeed the journey should march with the day, beginning and ending with its sun, to be the complete thing, the golden round, required of it. This makes that mind and body fare together, hand in hand, sharing the hope, the action, the fruition; finding equal sweetness in the languor of aching limbs at eve and in the first god-like intoxication of motion with braced muscle in the sun. For walk or ride take the mind over greater distances than a throbbing whirl with stiffening joints and cramped limbs through a dozen counties. Surely you seem to cover vaster spaces with Lavengro, footing it with gipsies or driving his tinker's cart across lonely commons, than with many a globe-trotter or steam-yachtsman with diary or log? And even that dividing line – strictly marked and rarely overstepped – between the man who bicycles and the man who walks, is less due to a prudent regard for personal safety of the one part than to an essential difference in minds.

There is a certain supernal, a deific, state of mind which may indeed be experienced in a minor degree, by any one, in the siesta part of a Turkish bath. But this particular golden glow of the faculties is only felt at its fulness after severe and prolonged exertion in the open air. "A man ought to be seen by the gods," says Marcus Aurelius, "neither dissatisfied with anything, nor complaining." Though this does not sound at first hearing an excessive demand to make of humanity, yet the gods, I fancy, look long and often for such a sight in these unblest days of hurry. If ever seen at all, 'tis when after many a mile in sun and wind – maybe rain – you reach at last, with the folding star, your destined rustic inn. There, in its homely, comfortable strangeness, after unnumbered chops with country ale, the hard facts of life begin to swim in a golden mist. You are isled from accustomed cares and worries – you are set in a peculiar nook of rest. Then old failures seem partial successes, then old loves come back in their fairest form, but this time with never a shadow of regret, then old jokes renew their youth and flavour. You ask nothing of the gods above, nothing of men below – not even their company. Tomorrow you shall begin life again: shall write your book, make your fortune, do anything; meanwhile you sit, and the jolly world swings round, and you seem to hear it circle to the music of the spheres. What pipe was ever thus beatifying in effect? You are aching all over, and enjoying it; and the scent of the limes drifts in through the window. This is undoubtedly the best and greatest country in the world; and none but good fellows abide in it.

> "Laud we the Gods,
> And let our crooked smokes climb to their nostrils
> From our blest altars."

"In the Deep Undergrowth"

Quarry Wood, not far from The Mount in Cookham Dene, was probably the place where Kenneth Grahame felt closest to nature and her small citizens. First discovered during his childhood years, this wood became the "mysterious mine for exploration" which he depicted in the third chapter of *The Wind in the Willows*, "The Wild Wood".

Here, beneath the towering old trees, their leaves forming a cooling shade from the summer sun, and their sturdy branches a protection from the harsh winter weather, dwelt many of the little creatures that peopled Grahame's story: moles, water rats, badgers, stoats, weasels and a rich variety of birds. In little hollows and on grassy mounds, far from the curiosity of human-kind, the animals could relax or play undisturbed, and a true nature lover like Kenneth Grahame could steal noiselessly into this domain and lie quietly hidden watching the magical spectacle performed before his very eyes.

In both summer and winter, Grahame spent countless hours in such "hidden places", and the intimate knowledge of nature that he absorbed is vividly reflected in his portrayal of "The Wild Wood". Here, as I noted in my Introduction, he found what became "the still centre" around which his book evolved.

Charles Fairbanks, a friend of Grahame's who spent some time with him at Cookham Dene, recalls one summer day when the author tried summoning a creature in Quarry Wood. "He used a most alluring whistle, as sweet and imperative as any pipe of Pan," says Fairbanks. "I know I'd have gone anywhere it called! But there was no response. After several calls he gave it up, remarking: 'There's a Water Rat down there, at least it's his home; he's quite a friend of mine. Evidently he's gone on some excursion – I shall hear about it one day.' ''

There can be no doubt that Kenneth Grahame not only had a deep affection for wild animals, but also wanted to understand animal-talk – indeed he may even have come to believe that he did. ''The Wild Wood'' chapter seems to be based on an uncanny – one might almost say un-human – knowledge of the working of tiny animals' minds and instincts. And once again we find that Grahame had written about his insight into ''animal land'', not once but twice, before he came to compose *The Wind in the Willows*.

The first occasion was in 1890 when he wrote ''A Wood-Land At Home'' for the *National Observer*. Strangely, this charming mixture of woodland idyll and animal tragedy was never published in the magazine, and might well have been lost altogether if Patrick Chalmers had not unearthed a proof copy when he was going through the author's papers. Its revelations about Grahame's attitudes towards small wild creatures, as well as its links with ''The Wild Wood'', are very enlightening.

An even more important example of his apparent ability to understand animal talk is to be found in an introduction he was commissioned to write for an edition of Sir Roger L'Estrange's *One Hundred Fables of Aesop*, published in 1899. Eleanor Graham has pin-pointed its importance: ''This he undertook chiefly because, looking back over the centuries through which the *Fables* had been published and read, he felt a strong desire to see justice done to the animals by showing how Aesop had misrepresented them in order to point his morals. It may well be that working over his foreword to the *Fables* set his own memories stirring, those myriad memories of the little animals he had watched through the years going about their own concerns. Yet his imagination was not stirred to creation point until he had his own child jogging at his elbow and asking for stories, for more and more stories – a child with whom he could share in delightful comradeship at last, his memories of the animals, so well observed . . .''

Quarry Wood near Cookham Dene, a childhood haunt that became the prototype for the Wild Wood.

This remarkable essay is tied all the closer to "The Wild Wood" because at its heart stands the figure of a strong and wise badger – that self-same Badger who, at the climax of the chapter, welcomes in the lost and frightened Mole and Rat from the snowbound world outside his front door.

* * *

A WOOD-LAND AT HOME

AFTER those nearly vertical rays outside, the copse, once its shelter is gained, is an instant relief and a most blessed refreshment. A little heaven of shade, it is stored with everything a sensible man can ask on a tropical day: everything, that is, but beer, which, indeed, must not be so much as thought of, if reason be to hold her seat in a distracted globe. In the open, the Lybian air not more adust, up to the dry lip of the gaping chalk-pit, is a stretch of sheep-cropped sward, and thereover the heated atmosphere broods flickering till the quiet distance is all a-jostle and a-quake; but here are peace, seclusion, a sweet-breathed wind, couch of bracken, swaying shelter of beechen green. Here might one lie and doze, and muse, and doze again, the most contented animal under the sun, the whole long, lazy afternoon – if only one could command the needful habit of mind. But to bring the green thought to the green shade – to go work-forgetting being world-forgot – holiday-making in rabbit-land, to take on a rabbit's considering-cap – that is just what none of us, slaves as we are of every tricksy maggot in the over-fermented brain, may look to do. Once here, for instance, I had meant to dismiss with a backward jerk of the thumb the disagreeable entity I had dragged up with me, and, casting the body's vesture, to commune trancedly with the woodland spirit, till it slipped its bark and leaf and blade, even as I my flesh and bones, and we twain were twain no more. But my petulant Ego will have none of it; he has a humour of aggressiveness today: and he takes the most disgusting way there is of showing it, by persistently recalling a certain past that I would resign to any dealer in marine stores on very easy terms.

All pasts are hateful – one or two distinctly more hateful than others; and an Ego that on a day like this goes on reminding you of your own peculiar burden is – to say the least – no gentleman. But I can pretend to take no notice: making believe very much, I can sprawl on the bracken, and seem to ignore him. He hates that. I hear him muttering and growling in my ear, but fainter – fainter – fainter! It is plain that I have fobbed him off for good.

Then . . . ! There is a rustle in the last year's leaves that still cling round the edge of the wood; the young bracken-shoots are quivering and shaking: and yet the rabbits – I have it from one of themselves – have all gone to an At-Home today! With a sinking heart I watch a tiny procession come forth into the open. Woe is me! I know the faces in it, every one. The bearers are dead days; bespangled some, and some in plain russet, and many draggled and smirched, but all averse and resolute, grimly set towards the lip of the chalk-pit. And the stark little forms they carry, I know them too. Old hopes all of them, some pathetically deformed, others of comelier build and hide and hue, but, of all, the gauzy, transparent wings are folded straight and close. Their hour has come. Stark and cold, with no banner nor march-music, but in sad undecorated silence, they are carried out for committal to the chalk-pit. I watch the vanguard pass, and without a sigh; schoolboy hopes these, comically misshapen, tawdry and crude in colour – let the pit receive them, and a good riddance! But those poor little corpses at their heel – *they* are tight and trim enough, some of them at least. And their pinions are brave and well set on, and might have borne them fast and far. Who left these stout young fledglings to perish? Starvation and neglect are ugly words, in truth. Is it even now too late? With downcast faces the bearers pace on, and the chalk-pit engulfs their burdens one by one.

Let them go. Who cares? This beechen shade would not be cooler, the brave summer day no longer by an hour, had every one of them lived to wing it in triumph up to the very sun. Achievement ever includes defeat: at best I should only have found myself where I am now – with a narrowing strip of sun and sward between me and the vast inevitable pit a-gape for us each and all. And the grapes are sour; and the hopes are dead; and the funeral is nearing its end. Only one little corpse is left; and the very bearers seem to beweep their trifling burden. Some hues of life seem even yet to flush the frail limbs and the delicate features; the glorious wings are still tinctured with an iris as of Paradise. Not that one! Let me keep that just a little longer! Surely it cannot be dead? Only yesterday I nursed its failing little frame awhile. Take all the others, only leave me that! In vain. The small bearers avert their faces, and the dainty ephemerid, involved in the common doom, follows its mates over the chalk-pit's edge into the still-unravined grave.

The sun is low by this time and strikes athwart: a cool wind wanders up the valley; the rabbits are dotting the neighbour field, intent on their evening meal; and – did somebody mention beer? or did I only dream it with the rest? It is time to have done with fancies and get back to a world of facts. If only one could! But that cry of the Portuguese Nun wails ever in the mind's ear: "I defy you to forget me utterly." Well, one can but try. It will be easier, now that they are really buried all. Hail and farewell to the short-lived dead! The pyre is out, the supreme valediction over and done.

* * *

ANIMAL-LAND

THE fable had its origin, we are given to understand, in a germ of politeness still lingering in the breast of the superior, or preaching, portion of humanity, who wished to avoid giving more pain than necessary when pursuing the inevitable task laid upon them by their virtues, of instructing the inferior and silent portion how to be – well, just a little less inferior, if they would only listen patiently to what they were told. It was also frankly admitted by many, that there were difficulties in getting a frivolous humanity to listen at all, unless one took a leaf from the book of that unprofitable rascal the story-teller, a spinner of webs for the sheer irridescence and gossamer-film and sparkle of the dainty thing itself; with no designs whatever upon fat, black flies, to be caught and held in its meshes. And so, with half a sigh, the preacher fell upon the element of fiction, and the fable was born. It would have been pleasanter, of course, to have told Smith to his face what a rogue he was, and Jones, what an idiot everybody thought him; but unfortunately there was no means of putting compulsion on Smith and Jones to attend. Again, it would have been quite easy to have got the Smiths and Joneses to sit round in a circle, while the theme was the folly of Robinson and the roguery of Jenkins; but Jenkins and Robinson might stroll in, arm-in-arm, in the middle, and the preacher who aimed at being a popular success knew that he must not only avoid all little unpleasantnesses, but also spin a web whose meshes were fine enough to catch and to hold, without undue obviousness, flies of every bulk, from Smith down to the recalcitrant Jenkins.

It is more probable that the thing had its roots in the fixed and firm refusal of the community from its very beginning, to allow any one of its members to go about calling any other one a fool or a rogue, ''of his own mere notion.'' If anybody has got to be put away for folly, or trounced for roguery, society has always told off some one to do it, and paid him a more or less adequate salary. The amateur has never been recognised nor countenanced, and though occasionally he may score a success for the moment, and set a convicted people beating their breasts in the streets, confessing their sins to each other at the street-corners, and making piles of their costly books and curios and precious ornaments in the market-place, sooner or later the old rule asserts itself, the paid policeman moves you on as before, and the forsaken and discredited amateur comes to hopeless grief.

What then was to be done? The inadequate policeman had to be supplemented, the amateur must somehow say his say. There was a certain moral cowardice in the means he hit upon. The friendly, tactful, unobstrusive beasts around him – could they not be seized upon and utilised to point the requisite moral? True, it would be no good to hold up their real characteristics for the public admonishment. The moment they were really studied they were seen to be so modest, so mutually helpful, so entirely free from vanity, affectation, and fads; so tolerant, uncomplaining, and determined to make the best of everything; and, finally, such adepts in the art of minding their own business, that it was evident a self-respecting humanity would not stand the real truth for a moment. But one could deal out the more prominent of human failings among them; one could agree, for argument's sake, that the peacock was to be vain, the wolf unregardful of his plighted work, the jackdaw a snob with a weakness for upper circles; and the thing was done. The Smiths and Joneses, instead of disputing the premises, fell into the trap; while the honest beasts, whose characters were thus meanly filched from them, instead of holding indignation-meetings, and passing resolutions of protest, as they might have done had they been merely human, took the nobler course of quietly continuing to mind their own business.

But though they acquiesced and submitted, it must not be thought that they did not feel and resent, very keenly indeed, the ungentlemanly manner in which they had been exploited, for moral purposes, by people with whom they only wished to live in mutual esteem and respect in a world in which there was plenty of room for both. When you meet a bird or a beast, and it promptly proceeds to move off, in an obviously different direction, without abuse indeed, or scurrility, or even reproach, but with a distinct intention of seeing as little of you as possible during the rest of the afternoon, you may be pretty sure it is thinking of Aesop's Fables. If only somebody would withdraw and apologise, and arrrange that things should be on the same footing as before!

Some beasts have gone so far as to take a leaf out of the book of the fabulist, and compile a volume of their own. Though humanity had behaved in a way to which they themselves would have scorned to stoop, that was no reason (they argued) why they should shun any moral lesson that was to be picked up, even from Man. A beast's life is so short, so eventful and precarious, that he is never above learning, never too proud to take a hint; more than all, he never thinks that what he doesn't know isn't worth knowing. I was allowed a glimpse at the book one afternoon, in a pine wood, when the world was hot and sleepy, and the beasts had dined well. But I could not get permission to take it away, and, as

I was sleepy too, I can only half recollect a scant fable or two out of that rich treasure-house; and somehow I have never been able to happen upon that pine wood again.

Naturally enough with creatures who live by rule and order and inherited precept, the inconsequential and irregular habits of man afford much food for beast-reflection. Here is a fable (by a monkey apparently) which touches on this puzzling aspect of humanity.

THE APE AND THE CHILD IN THE LEGHORN HAT

A frolicsome ape, who in much careless ease inhabited a lordly mansion in Regent's Park, lounged up one afternoon to certain bars, on the other side of which selected specimens of humanity were compelled to promenade each day for the instruction and diversion of philosophic apes. A little maid in a Leghorn hat having timidly approached the bars, her large fat mother, shaking her imperiously by the shoulder, ordered her to observe the pitty ickle monkey, so mild and so gentle, and give it a piece of her bun at once, like a good, kind, charitable ickle girl. The small maiden, though herself extremely loth, proffered her bun to the ape, who possessed himself of it with a squeal of delight, and bit her finger to the bone as well: for he had bitten nothing more juicy and succulent than a neighbour's tail for a whole week past; and tails are but grisly things at the best. But the large, fat mother, falling upon the already shrieking little girl, shook and cuffed her unmercifully, protesting that of all the naughty, tiresome, self-willed little trollops, and that never, never, never would she take her a-pleasuring again.

Moral

Parents of the human species have an altogether singular and unaccountable method of rearing their young. Yet they grow up somehow, nevertheless, and often become quite good and useful citizens: so there may be something in it, and it's a lesson to us not to be proud and think we know everything.

Here is another (by a dog this time) based on the same characteristic, but written from a slightly different and more doggy point of view.

THE DOG, THE CHILD, AND THE MOON

A child sat on the nursery floor and cried for the moon, which was shining so temptingly through the window. A conscientious dog who was strolling by, and had been wanting sorely to bay at the moon all the evening, because he had a bad pain in his inside that kept telling him to do it, only he was mighty afeared of being kicked, sat down beside the infant, and, with the sole remark that circumstances were too strong for him, lifted his snout. Then the night was filled with music, till even the face of the moon wore a pained expression; and the dog felt the pain in his inside trickling away through his ribs. Attracted by the outcry, the mother hastened to the room, and smacked the child soundly for its folly and unreasonableness. But she patted and praised the dog, who was sitting severely on his tail, and called him a noble, sympathetic fellow, who could not see others in trouble without being moved to share their distress. Then the dog swaggered out of the room feeling good all over, and resolving that next morning he would dig a hole in the geranium-bed large enough to bury the moon itself.

Moral

You never can tell with exactness how human beings will act, under any conditions. Therefore when you want to howl at the moon, or do anything contraband, badly enough, better go and do it and get it over. You can but be kicked, and you probably won't be, and you will get rid of the bad pain in your inside.

Then there was that fable – and the one about – and the other one where – and then that very naughty one which – but it is time to pull up, as I promised faithfully not to. How it all comes back to me as I write! The cushion of moss and pine-needles, the song of the streamlet hard by, the squirrel perched half-way up a tree-trunk and chattering, "Do read him that one about –" and the jay, who was turning over the leaves, looking round and saying, "O you shut up! This is my copy he's looking at, and it opens at all the right places!" The rabbits sat round in a ring, silent and large-eyed, with just a flicker passing over their ever-unrestful noses. They will always come to listen to a story, however old and hackneyed, and never open their mouths except to say, "Now another, please!" The badger, who, as the biggest member

present, ought to have been doing the honours, and knew it, sat
and scratched himself, and looked crossly at the jay. He wanted to
say something cutting, but knew the jay was his master at repar-
tee. Then the woodland muttered its spell, and a drowsiness crept
over us. When I awoke the badger's chair was vacant, the rabbits
were but a rustle in the bracken, the squirrel and the jay but a
quiver in a tree-top and a glint of blue against a distant copse.

Well! The story-teller, the gossamer-web-spinner, has come to
his own by this time, and the fabulist, who started with such a
flourish, has long ceased to mount his tub. Even while these very
fables were in course of writing, the axe was being laid to the root
of the tree, and a whimsical fellow, with his tongue in his cheek,
was compiling the ''Arabian Nights''. In this matter humanity,
though just as liable as the individual to its temporary fits of
affectation, knows what it wants and sees that it gets it, and never
troubles to justify its selection by argument. Did it care to do so,
it might contend that people, by diligent attention to morals and
rubbing in of applications, had become quite too good for
anything, and the fables had done their work so thoroughly that
now the time had arrived for a little relaxation, honestly earned.
Or it might argue, on the other hand, that the job had proved too
tough a one, that the story which posed as an obvious index to
personal conduct had got to be a bore and a nuisance, and that it
was much nicer to be frankly bad and shameless and abandoned,
and read fiction. But humanity, in the mass, never argues – and
rightly; and the reader can please himself with whichever theory
he likes, sure of this at least, that the story henceforth will be
tolerated only for itself, that the fable has had its day and ceased to
be.

But a method may expire, and its output yet remain that un-
defined thing, attained by neither prayer nor fasting – a classic.
(Indeed, so long as you are a part of this earth's old crust, you
must generally wait till you are a stratum before people will begin
paying attention to you and calling you nice names.) There are in
literature men, women, and beasts, who survive owing to fidelity
in portraiture to the natural type. There are equally men, women,
and beasts, who live from their very deviation from the real thing

– fresh and captivating creations with rules of their own. These
are the folk who people the world of fairy-tale, heraldry, and fable;
and many such village communities flourish in classic-land.
Vitality – that is the test; and, whatever its components, mere
truth is not necessarily one of them. A dragon, for instance, is a
more enduring animal than a pterodactyl. I have never yet met
any one who really believed in a pterodactyl; but every honest
person believes in dragons – down in the back-kitchen of his consciousness. And every honest person believes that the fable-
people exist, or existed, somewhere – not on this planet, perhaps,
since personal experience must be allowed its place when evidence has to be weighed, but – well, the Census Department
has never yet overhauled the Dog-Star.

And this classic is here given forth in the brave old seven-
teenth-century version of Sir Roger L'Estrange, who wrote, by a
happy gift, in the very language (we feel sure) that the Fable-
beasts now talk among themselves in Fable-land. Modern ren-
derings, with one eye on the anxious parent and the other on the
German governess, have often achieved an impotence of English
that increases our admiration of a tongue that can survive such
mishandling, and still remain the language of men. "Insipid
Twittle-Twattles," to use L'Estrange's own phrase. A Royalist
politician and a fluent and copious pamphleteer, he had graduated
in the right school for work wherein one hard-hitting word must
needs supply the place of whole page or long-drawn paragraph in
the less restricted methods by which the human conscience now
insists on being approached. In the sad case of the Lion, the Bear,
and the Fox, a modern version draws the moral in these satisfactory if hardly stimulating terms:

"Those who fight with each other lose all, and give others
the chance of enriching themselves."

Dear me, do they really? Lay this alongside of our politician's,
and with a snap and a bite he has you by the leg.

"'Tis the fate of all *Gotham Quarrels*, when fools go together
by the ears, to have knaves run away with the stakes."

Again, – "A certain Jackdaw was so proud and ambitious that,
&c.," bleats and trickles our modern version. "A Daw that had

a mind to be sparkish,'' says L'Estrange, saving his breath for his story. Yet he is not merely forcible, terse, and arresting. With what a prettiness of phrase he puts (in his preface) the case for the Fable! ''What cannot be done by the dint of Authority, or Persuasion, in the Chappel, or in the Closet, must be brought about by the Side-Wind of a Lecture from the Fields and the Forrests.'' And there is a touch both quiet and appealing in his account of the Tailless Fox, and his efforts to get level again with Society: ''. . . But however, for the better countenance of the scandal, he got the Master and Wardens of the Foxes Company to call a Court of Assistants, where he himself appeared, and made a Learned Discourse upon the Trouble, the Uselessness, and the Indecency, of Foxes wearing Tails.''

But, as I have said, it is in his Beast-talk that our politician (naturally enough) excels:

''But as they were entering upon the Dividend, 'Hands off,' says the Lion. 'This part is mine by the Privilege of my Quality; this, because I'll have it in spite of your Teeth; this, again, because I took most pains for't; and if you dispute the Fourth, we must e'en Pluck a Crow about it.' '' In the ''Wolf and the Lamb,'' '' 'Nay,' says t'other, 'you'll never leave your chopping of Logick, till your Skin's turned over your Ears, as your Father's was, a matter of Six Months ago, for prating at this sawcy rate.' ''

L'Estrange may have had his faults of diction: faults of excess, of violence, of recurrent effort for the explosive phrase, wherein we get, indeed, the telling snapshot effect, but somehow hear the click of the Kodak as well. Yet his version remains the one version, and these are not the times in which we may expect to get another. It is more than doubtful whether Aesop would have approved of it; and yet, for good or for evil, it is the ultimate version!

Those green back-garden doors that lead to the trim classic plots – they are opened but rarely now-a-days! For they are a trifle warped, and their paint swollen, and they stick and jam, and one can find neither time nor effort for the necessary tug. But once inside this particular door – if one takes the pains – how one is possessed by the inhabitants, their surroundings, their ways, and their points of view! Emerging, one really expects to meet them at every corner, to be hailed by them, to put the natural question and get the appropriate answer. One forgets, for the moment, that the real four-legged or feathered fellows one encounters are sullen, rancorous, and aggrieved – have a book of their own, in fine, a version in which it is *we* who point the moral and adorn the tale!

"A Kind-Hearted Gentleman"

"Mr. Badger," the fourth chapter in *The Wind in the Willows*, introduces us to perhaps the most stalwart, reliable and likeable character in the whole story. There have been hints about him in earlier chapters; Rat, for instance, speaks of him in the most complimentary terms, calling him the "best of fellows", but insisting that he is a person who likes to keep himself to himself. "He hates Society," Rat tells Mole, "and invitations, and dinner, and all that sort of thing." Even when Mole persists in his demands to be allowed to meet this elusive figure, Rat remains adamant. "He's so very shy," he says, "he'd be sure to be offended."

So it is that the two friends only meet Badger when they become lost in a snow storm in the Wild Wood and accidentally stumble upon his front door. In their distress they have no alternative but to seek the solitary grey animal's hospitality – and Badger proves to be an immediately welcoming and generous host.

Kenneth Grahame tells us that Badger seemed, "by all accounts, to be such an important personage," and although he was not often seen, seemed "to make his unseen influence felt by everybody about the place." These singularly appropriate words also describe Grahame's own importance in the area along the banks of the River Thames where he lived from 1906 onwards, first at Mayfield in Cookham Dene, then at the farm known as Boham's in Blewbury, near Didcot and finally, at Church Cottage, Pangbourne.

In the years following the publication of *The Wind in the*

Mayfield, the house at Cookham Dene where the
Grahames lived from 1906 until 1910.

Willows, Grahame preferred to keep himself to himself, and although he was often seen walking about the district, did not encourage conversation. He was, however, ever ready to help in local affairs when he believed he might be of assistance – ''he was its stimulus, its example and its consoler'', according to Patrick Chalmers – but resented unexpected callers who came to lionise him. In fact, he loved solitude, and there is much of him to be found in the character of Mr. Badger. Peter Green has explained how Grahame's penchant for being on his own had played an important part in the creation of his masterpiece:

''What he had produced was the fruit of a certain conflict in the mind: first, the tension between his banking career and his Hesperidean dreams; second, the struggle for mastery between

the 'Fellow that Goes Alone' and Mr. Grahame the family man.
Both of these antitheses could be subsumed under the general
heading of Desire versus Duty. But his retirement had auto-
matically destroyed the first; and *The Wind in the Willows* had
largely resolved the second. He had sufficient income; he had lost
his dream; there was now no driving impulse for him to go on
writing. Instead, he sat by the fire and read Milton, or tramped for
hours (the old, well-tried anodyne) over the Berkshire Downs.''

To Kenneth Grahame solitude was not a negative state –
although there was certainly an element of escape in it – but as
Eleanor Graham has noted, it created in him a quite positive
happiness, ''a state in which his perceptions – his looking and
hearing – were more acute and his comprehension more penetrat-
ing . . . In solitude came a sense he greatly prized, of being at one
with wild nature.''

The parallels between Grahame and Mr. Badger become
increasingly evident in the chapter which bears his name, and
continue later on in the book. But once more the author had
anticipated himself: in an essay which is as much about his
own character as that of the badger – ''The Fellow That Walks
Alone.'' Written, apparently, during one of his weekends at
Cookham Dene, it was not actually published until July 1913
when the editor of his old school magazine, the *St. Edward's
School Chronicle*, requested a contribution from its now famous
old boy for the Jubilee Commemoration Number. Grahame
obliged with this revealing essay extracted from his files.

Kenneth Grahame also drew on another earlier essay in
composing the chapter about Mr. Badger. This concerned the
door to his home which had proved such a welcome sight to the
snow-bound Mole and Rat. The model here was to be found in an
item entitled, simply, ''The Barn Door'' which he had contributed to the *National Observer* in October 1893. The door in
question was a real one he knew on the barn of a farmer named
Mr. Caudwell in Blewbury, and in the essay Grahame manages to
convey the same feelings of anxiety mixed with the sense of
security represented by such a door, that he later evoked in ''Mr.
Badger''.

* * *

THE FELLOW THAT WALKS ALONE

THOSE who have browsed among the pages of Caxton's *Golden Legend* – a story-book of much fascination – may remember how it is told, in a passage concerning the boyhood of a certain English saint – Edmund, Archbishop and Confessor – that on a day when the boy was by himself in a meadow, "sodeynlye there apperyd tofore hym a fayr chylde in whyte clothynge which sayd, 'Hayle, felowe that goest alone'."

Local considerations themselves should make us cherish the memory of this Edmund with a certain tenderness; for he was born at the pleasant town of Abingdon, that sits among its lush water-meadows and almost catches the chimes down the stream from the not so distant Oxford towers; and he "went to Oxenforde to scole", as of course a good saint should; and many a time he must have ridden out over Grandpont and along the old raised "Cawsy" – still there under the road – to visit his home and his good mother who was thought worthy to have inscribed on her tomb that she was the "flower of widows". Also he "dwellyd long after at Oxenforde" and "Teddy", the last of the old Halls, is said to perpetuate his name. But specially we should envy him his white vision in the meadow; for which he should be regarded as the patron saint of all those who of set purpose choose to walk alone, who know the special grace attaching to it, and ever feel that somewhere just ahead, round the next bend perhaps, the White Child may be waiting for them.

For Nature's particular gift to the walker, through the semi-mechanical act of walking – a gift no other form of exercise seems to transmit in the same high degree – is to set the mind jogging, to make it garrulous, exalted, a little mad maybe – certainly creative and suprasensitive, until at last it really seems to be out-side of you and as it were talking to you, while you are talking back to it. Then everything gradually seems to join in, sun and the wind, the white road and the dusty hedges, the spirit of the

season, whichever that may be, the friendly old earth that is pushing forth life of every sort under your feet or spell-bound in death-
like winter trance, till you walk in the midst of a blessed company, immersed in a dream-talk far transcending any possible
human conversation. Time enough, later, for that – across the
dinner table, in smoking-room armchairs; here and now, the
mind has shaken off its harness, is snorting and kicking up heels
like a colt in a meadow. Not a fiftieth part of all your happy
imaginings will you ever, later, recapture, note down, reduce to
dull inadequate words; but meantime the mind has stretched itself
and had its holiday. But this emancipation is only attained in
solitude, the solitude which the unseen companions demand
before they will come out and talk to you; for, be he who may, if
there is another fellow present, your mind has to trot between
shafts.

A certain amount of ''shafts'', indeed, is helpful, as setting the
mind more free; and so the high road, while it should always give
way to the field path when choice offers, still has this particular
virtue, that it takes charge of you – your body, that is to say. Its
hedges hold you in friendly steering-reins, its milestones and
finger-posts are always on hand, with information succinct and
free from frills; and it always gets *somewhere*, sooner or later. So
you are nursed along your way, and the mind may soar in cloudland and never need to be pulled earthwards by any string. But
this is as much company as you ought to require, the comradeship of the road you walk on, the road which will look after you
and attend to such facts as must not be overlooked. Of course the
best sort of walk is the one on which it doesn't matter twopence
whether you get anywhere at all at any time or not; and the
second best is the one on which the hard facts of routes, times, or
trains give you nothing to worry about. And this is perhaps the
only excuse for the presence of that much-deprecated Other
Fellow – that you can put all that sort of thing on to him. For the
world is fortunately well-furnished with fellows who really like
looking up Bradshaw, and paying bills, and taking charge
generally; and it is wise to keep some such a man within easy hail.
But spiritually he will be of little use, even if he were the angel

that walked with Tobias.

Much converse will he have, too, with shy bird and furtive little beast, the fellow that walks alone. I seem to have noticed a different expression in the eye of bird or animal at one's solitary approach, from the way it looks at you when there are two or three of you about. In the first case it seems to say wistfully, "This *may* be a pal!" In the second, "This is certainly a conspiracy!" and acts accordingly. As for adventures, if they are the game you hunt, everyone's experience will remind him that the best adventures of his life were pursued and achieved, or came suddenly to him unsought, when he was alone. For company too often means compromise, discretion, the choice of the sweetly reasonable. It is difficult to be mad in company; yet but a touch of lunacy in action will open magic doors to rare and unforgettable experiences.

But all these are only the by-products, the casual gains, of walking alone. The high converse, the high adventures, will be in the country of the mind.

* * *

THE BARN-DOOR

AT this time of the waning year, a stroll through the woods may force one to own up to and acknowledge the season's conventional melancholy. The recognition is annoying: one so much prefers to find convention in the wrong. But on that particular morning the spirit of melancholy walked abroad, too potent to be denied. My only chance seemed to be resolutely to reject the application to my own condition, and, with a touch of joyance, to reflect instead, as I sauntered along, on the exceeding parlous state of my friends.

I had mentally run through the sorry catalogue ('tis no long one), and damned them all most heartily, ere I quitted the wood, and sought the lee-side of the great barn, to kindle a fresh pipe in its shelter; and it was as I raised my eyes from the expiring match that the mute, sad decoration of the barn-door struck me with some touch of remorse. The Tuscan poet, led by the Mantuan Shade, saw below many a friend of old time planted in fire, in mud, in burning marl, *ove i bolliti faceano alte strida*; but to come across them nailed in rows on a barn-door, seems to have been specially reserved for me. I had handled them severely, perhaps, during my meditations in the wood: but certainly I neither expected nor desired to find them all thus transfixed, with plumage smirched and fur bedraggled, wasted by the sun and rain. You now, with the soft white throat and delicate paws, all sinuous grace and sleek beauty when alive – so it has come to this? And yet, my fair lady, you were once the arrantest of blood-suckers, and drained the life out of many a one in your merry career. What? They were only silly rabbits! Well, perhaps they were a brainless lot, not greatly to be pitied; but the wheel has gone round, and now it is the rabbits' turn to laugh. And your fine neighbour of the tawny back, with the vivid glint of turquoise-blue on either wing: the handsomest spark in our English woods – I was thinking of him only just now. A loud-voiced fellow rather; fond of showing-off and cutting a dash; with a weakness for a lord; altogether not quite the best form perhaps; – and yet, what a good sort of chap he was, after all! Now, his strident accents are hushed, his gay feathers drop one by one. What strange fate has fixed him cheek by jowl with our friend of the solemn face and round eyes? Of him we were wont to see little, during daylight hours; but after dinner, when he flapped around seeking his prey! – well, they are all now in the same silent row, the bore as well as the chatterer. You dingy fellow with the hooky beak and cruel claws – you knocked some fur out of *my* back once, old boy, though I just managed to wriggle down a friendly burrow in time; I don't grudge *you* to the barn-door – nor yet this half-dozen of rats, rodent no longer. But in the ranks I still espy another friend or two for whom this fate seems unduly hard.

And yet one might come to a worse end. The merry winds still sing in our plumage – what is left of it; the kindly sun still warms us through, sounds of the cheery farm-yard are ever in our ears, light and life and song surround us still, and nothing any longer has power to hurt. Does any one want a lock of my hair, a gay feather from my plumage? 'Tis at your service; to weave into your nest, or enshrine in a locket – all's one to me – help yourself. Was I a churl, haply, in life? a mean and grasping niggard? No more liberal fellow now decorates a barn-door. Proud was I, perhaps – stand-offish, given to airs? There's no pride about me any longer. Your barn-door is a mighty leveller, and clears the mind of cant and prejudice. Why was hanging in chains ever condemned as a relic of barbarism? It is civility itself! Let us swing and creak in the wind, and brother call to brother across the barren moor, till the elements shred and take us piecemeal.

Yet the human majority, by some such instinct as that which drags the wounded rabbit to his hole, shrinks ever from uplifted exposure such as this. "Out of sight" is still their cry: "only let it be somewhere out of sight, once we are worn and old and dropping to pieces!" The burden of Brer Rabbit's appeal to his tormentor was, whatever he did, not to fling him in "dat brier-patch"; and humanity leaves to the fates an exceeding wide choice, so long as only they are not nailed up on that barn-door.

Perhaps, then, my poor friends are not entirely happy in their unsought publicity. Might it not be a kindly act on my part to give their poor remains a decent burial? To scatter just that gift of a little dust which shall bring to their unquiet shades release and repose? I owe them some sort of reparation for my hard thoughts concerning them half an hour ago, when I never dreamt of finding them gibbeted here. And yet – a sudden suspicion chills the blood. Were it not wise to get away quietly, but swiftly, while time yet serves for retreat? For the Grim Old Keeper who fixed them there – may he not be lurking somewhere hard by – with a mind, perhaps, to seize me and nail me up alongside the rest?

5

"A Long Day's Outing"

The drama of being lost in the snow until he is found by Rat, has a profound effect on Mole, and by chapter five, "Dulce Domum", he has reached some important conclusions about himself. Kenneth Grahame tells us, "As he hurried along, eagerly anticipating the moment when he would be at home again among the things he knew and liked, the Mole saw clearly that he was an animal of tilled field and hedgerow, linked to the ploughed furrow, the frequented pasture, the lane of evening lingerings, the cultivated garden-plot. For others the asperities, the stubborn endurance, or the clash of actual conflict, that went with Nature in the rough; he must be wise, must keep to the pleasant places in which his lines were laid and which held adventure enough, in their way, to last for a lifetime."

There are echoes here from one of Kenneth Grahame's very earliest essays, "By a Northern Furrow," which is the first identified contribution he made to the *St. James' Gazette*, in December 1888. The item was clearly inspired by walks the author had taken over the Berkshire Downs, and in his biography of Grahame, Peter Green has made a strong case through it for identifying Mole with the author. This is his contention:

"Grahame can be more nearly identified with Mole than any other of his characters: the patient, tunnelling, laborious Mole who suddenly bursts through into the sunlight and the leisurely life of the River. Like Grahame, he is tactful, wide-eyed, a little naive, content to play Watson to Ratty's Holmes; like Grahame again, he develops a violent, aching nostalgia for his old home –

Church Cottage, Pangbourne, Kenneth Grahame's last home. He moved here from Blewbury in 1924 and died on 6th July, 1932.

and goes back to it.* Mole's moments of self-analysis could be applied with equal justice to his creator.''

As I have shown earlier, it is possible to see Grahame in several

* Kenneth Grahame has provided an interesting footnote to this particular part of Mole's story. In 1919, a Professor G. T. Hill of London University wrote to him enquiring who had looked after Mole End while its owner was away sharing adventures with Rat, Badger and Toad. As this is one of the very few instances where Grahame enlarged on an aspect of his work, his reply to Professor Hill, ''Mr. Mole's Char-Mouse,'' which was written on September 24, 1919, is reprinted in the Appendix to this book.

of his characters, and indeed there is probably something of him in each, for the whole book is nothing if not an expression of his own yearning for the freedom of a life close to nature. ''By a Northern Furrow'' also has certain elements of ''Dulce Domum'' in its picture of little folk tramping the streets of a village (as do Mole and Rat) and in its imaginative reconstruction of a by-gone era (*vide* the field-mouse's capture by a Barbary corsair).

Another early essay is linked to this chapter, as Patrick Chalmers has noted in his biography during the course of a dis-cussion about the critical attention accorded to *The Wind in the Willows* over the years. ''Among the countless notices, British and American,'' he writes, ''the most-quoted-from chapter seems to be 'Wayfarers All' – the wander-lust of the swallows and later, of the Sea Rat. That chapter, and also its antithesis, 'Dulce Domum,' the Mole's tearful *heimweh* for his own 'shabby, dingy little place, not like – your cosy quarters – or Toad's beautiful hall – or Badger's great house – but it was my own little home – .' And reading these extracts, I am reminded of an essay that the author wrote thirteen years earlier in which he combines a Mole End, where he himself plays Mole, and an Odyssey in which the part of the Sea Rat (or Ulysses) is taken by a respectable member of the Baltic Exchange who wore 'drab spats all the year round'. It is a beautiful story and it is called 'The Iniquity of Oblivion' . . . it mixes the essential salts of 'Dulce Domum' and 'Wayfarers All' much as a chemist, or the 'Red Gods', mix a medicine.''

Such is the importance of ''The Iniquity of Oblivion'', which Grahame actually contributed to the notorious Victorian magazine, *The Yellow Book*, in October 1895, yet never collected among his works. He in fact wrote half a dozen pieces for this remarkable, short-lived periodical which now has a place in literary history because of its associations with Oscar Wilde and Aubrey Beardsley. At first sight it may seem very strange that a conservative figure like Kenneth Grahame should have contributed to such a radical journal: but it is true to say that his thinking was often far from orthodox, and he could on occasions be a prophet expressing controversial ideas long before their appointed time.

* * *

BY A NORTHERN FURROW

UP there, on the breezy top of the downs, the turf is virgin still to the share; the same turf that was trodden by the hurrying feet of Saxon levies ere they clashed with the Danish invader on yonder ridge. But down in the valley they shelter, the conquering plough has sped and swayed for centuries; and here, where this great shoulder merges into the fields with a gentler incline, it has gone out and made conquest; breasted the hill behind a double team, and made this spur captive. This year its turn has come late, and the furrows still gleam unbroken, touched each, on the side the share has polished, with warm light from the low red winter's sun. The stillness all around, the absence of chirping and singing life, the slight frost that holds the air, all seem silently to plead for a good word on behalf of a season that rarely gets one. After all, these brief sunless days, this suspended action of the year, impose restful conditions which those whose minds are in proper harmony with Nature only too gladly accept. Like the earth beneath us, we silently renew our forces for the coming awakening of life in nature and action in men; taking the while somewhat sad account of the past year's words and deeds, which, vital enough as they may have seemed at their doing and saying, none the less surely now strew our path with their withered leaves, rustling with recollections. We, who for our sins are town dwellers when the summer sun lights up gloomy squares and dusty streets, chafe at every sunlit day that passes as worse than wasted. Are we equally quick to miss and to long for the enforced repose of a winter with nature?

Meanwhile, leaning on the gate, it is pleasant to look upon a piece of work honestly done as well as it could be. No truer furrow could the divine herdsman himself have driven, when the fingers that had swept the lyre on Olympus were laid on the rude plough stilts, and the slow-plodding oxen, the very inanimate wood and iron, were stirred and thrilled by the virtue that went out of a god.

> When by Zeus relenting the mandate was revoked,
> Sentencing to exile the bright Sun-god,
> Mindful were the ploughmen of who the steer had yoked,
> Who; and what a track showed the upturned sod!

This at least he was good to do, the god turned thrall: to make his ''drudgery divine'' by perfection; to tend Admetus's sheep so that never should one be missed at folding-time, even as he herded the ''broad foreheaded oxen of the Sun'' on the trackless asphodel meadows; to drive his furrows straight and true, as when with his huntress sister he sent his silvery shafts one after the other clanging to the mark.

But the Delian suggestion jars on us as with a sense of incongruity, and recalls us to ourselves and our chill surroundings. Under modern culture our minds have become cosmopolitan in the widest sense; they range and possess not only the world that is, but that has been. Florentines we are perhaps, and encounter Beatrice with her salutation by the way; or we ride with Tannhäuser to Rome, with burden of sweet strange sin. When the summer sun is high we know and hail the Pythian one, the far darter: and the old Pan still pipes to us at Mapledurham or in Hurley backwater. Only when winter has us fast do we truly feel our kinship with the Scandinavian toilers of old time, who knew life to be a little space in which to do great deeds, a struggle with Nature and inclement seasons and the mightier unseen power of hostile fates. Such were our fathers, fighting nature for eight months of the year, wresting a hard sustenance from her by force, seeing in the iron sky above only another force that had to be combated also; and a tinge of this feeling in our minds is their heritage to us, and pricks us like a conscience when our imaginations would fain stray in Socratic myrtle-groves or *gelidis in volubus Hemi*.

The warping influence of toil and stress of weather, common heritage of the north, shows itself so clearly in the pictures of the

Northern or Flemish school as to give us a feeling towards them that we do not experience in inspecting other examples of early art. Some of the tender pity we might feel for the toil-worn face of a poor relation smites across us at sight of some of their homely Madonnas, pallid and drawn in face, bowed and warped in figure, only very human: the mothers and sisters of their painters. Most of all, their St. Christophers seem to epitomise their own history – the rude gigantic disproportioned figures, rough hewn as the staff that supports them, struggling to stem the torrent and bear the bright boy-Saviour to the shore. They, too, carried their divine burden safe to land, but the struggle was sore, and its marks are imprinted on their work.

Pain, and toil, and suffering, whether from fate or man's brutality, runs like an under song through these pictures of the North; and it is our fellowship with these pains, these common sorrows, small or great, that is the enduring tie, the touch that kins us. A Flemish Massacre of the Innocents which I once saw in a Continental gallery has made a more enduring impression on me than any carefully composed apposition of naked men's and children's legs and arms could do. It is a still dull frosty winter's afternoon, with a haze in the air and ice on the pond and puddles of the little village. School is over, and the children are returning to their low-roofed houses in the little street; and though the place is very poor, they are warmly clad in their mittens and gaiters and wraps. Suddenly round the corner and down the street ride a group of gaunt and hard-faced spearmen, who fall on the children in a passionless businesslike way, clambering up water-butts and spouts, giving each other a shoulder, to get at those who escape into the houses. And the mothers – clumsy, awkward, loving women – amazedly run hither and thither, begging a little pity with grotesque extravagant gesticulations, the best they can command. Day by day they have wrapped their little ones warmly for school: what hope or promise can they see now, in their blank dismay and crying appealing terror? For such as these remains no joyful vision of their innocents triumphing, as in Holman Hunt's great picture, hailed by the infant Saviour as his first fruits, marching, a mystical priesthood.

So, too, the many small domestic touches appeal especially to our home loving natures: as when, in our own National Gallery, the Virgin sits alone, under no silken canopy, backed by no gracious enwreathment of olive or myrtle, but with homely oaken chest and cupboard about her; while, seen through the small window, couples stroll home in the evening light – the evening that brings all home; not knowing that for them a new hope has arisen, a new solace and comfort at the end of a weary day.

But chiefest of all, to me – watching the tender evening light on these furrows, and thinking of the toil-worn bowed figure that drew them, and has done for many a year, he and his friendly companion-beasts – appears, in its severe outline, Holbein's drawing of the gaunt ploughman, hardly better clad than his grim and terrible companion, who takes from him the guidance of the horses. ''Of this other picture,'' says Ruskin, ''the meaning is plainer, and far more beautiful. The husbandman is old and gaunt, and has passed his days, not in speaking, but in pressing the iron into the ground. And the payment for his life's work is that he is clothed in rags, and his feet are bare on the clods; and he has no hat, but the brim of a hat only, and his long unkempt grey hair comes through. But all the air is full of warmth and peace; and beyond his village church there is, at last, light indeed. His horses lag in the furrow, and his own limbs totter and fail; but one comes to help him. 'It is a long field,' says Death; 'but we'll get to the end of it today – you and I.' ''

Here pain and suffering are hardly felt. It is Death the serene and gracious, ''Death the Friend.'' It is Tennyson's Death, who

> Like a friend's voice in a distant field
> Approaching through the darkness, called.

Or Whitman's –

> Undulate round the world, serenely arriving, arriving;
> In a day or a night, to all, to each,
> Sooner or later, beautiful Death.

But it is death none the less; we must go to the southern Botticelli for the glad poetry of Birth – of the birth of Venus, and of Spring with the air full of mysterious blossoms; of Christ, with the angels encircling the lowly shed with enraptured, almost delirious dance of joy.

To the northern artist, life is a no less precious possession: rather dearer from the more conscious presence of "the Shadow waiting with the keys". As Mr. Pater has it, "it is with a rush of home sickness that the thought of death presents itself. He would remain at home for ever on the earth if he could; as it loses its colour and the senses fail, he clings ever closer to it; but since the mouldering of bones and flesh must go on to the end, he is careful of charms and talismans, that may chance to have some friendly power in them when the inevitable shipwreck comes."

So, from no love of them, but rather with a shuddering fear, he must be busy with all emblems of mortality: often unconsciously, as children play at funerals; or as the plough here, speeding on its fertilising mission, turns up bones and skulls which have rested "under the drums and tramplings of three conquests."

* * *

THE INIQUITY OF OBLIVION

A MAN I know is fond of asking the irritating question – and in putting it he regards neither age nor sex, neither ancient friendship nor the rawest nodding acquaintance – "Did you ever forget an invitation to dinner?"

Of course the denial is prompt, passionate, and invariable. There are few crimes of which one would not rather be accused than this. He who cannot summon up the faintest blush at the recollection of having once said "Season", when no money had passed between him and the Railway Company whose guest he was for the moment, of having under-stated his income for purposes of taxation, or of having told his wife he was going to church, and then furtively picked up a fishing-rod as he passed through the hall, will colour angrily at the most innocent suggestion of a single possible lapse of memory regarding an invitation to dinner. But, none the less, every one finds it a little difficult to meet the natural rejoinder: "How do you know?"

Indeed, no other reply than painful silence is possible. To say, "Because I do," is natural enough and frequently quite conclusive of further argument; still, it can hardly be called a reasoned refutation. The fact is, you *don't* know, and you cannot know. Your conviction that you do is based, first, on some sort of idea that you are bound to recollect, sooner or later, anything that you may have forgotten: an argument that only requires to be stated to display its fallacy; secondly, on a vague belief that a deflection of so flagrant a character must inevitably be brought home to you by an incensed host or hostess – a theory that makes no allowance for the blissful sense of injury and offended pride, the joy of brooding over a wrong, which is one of the chief pleasures left to humanity. No, one doesn't know, and one can't know: and the past career of the most self-satisfied of us is doubtless littered with the debris of forgotten invitations.

Of course invitations, being but a small part of life, and not – as some would imply with their practice – its chief end, must be taken to stand here for much besides. One has only to think of the appalling amount of book-lore one has "crammed" in days gone by, and of the pitiful fragments that survive, to realise that facts, deeds, achievements, experiences numberless, may just as well have been hurried along the dusty track to oblivion. And once it has been fairly brought home to us that we have entirely forgotten any one thing – why, the gate is open. It is clear we may just as easily have forgotten hundreds.

This lamentable position of things was specially forced upon me, some time ago, by a certain persistent dream that used to wing its way to my bedside, not once or twice, but coming a dozen times, and always (I felt sure at the time) from out the Ivory Portal. First, there would be a sense of snugness, of cushioned comfort, of home-coming. Next, a gradual awakening to consciousness in a certain little room, very dear and familiar, sequestered in some corner of the more populous and roaring part of London: solitary, the world walled out, but full of a brooding sense of peace and of possession. At times I would make my way there, unerringly, through the wet and windy streets, climb the well-known staircase, open the ever-welcoming door. More often I was there already, ensconced in the most comfortable chair in the world, the lamp lit, the fire glowing ruddily. But always the same feeling of a home-coming, of the world shut out, of the ideal encasement. On the shelves were a few books – a very few – but just the editions I had sighed for, the editions which refuse to turn up, or which poverty glowers at on alien shelves. On the walls were a print or two, a woodcut, an etching – not many. Old loves, all of them, apparitions that had flashed across the field of view in sale-rooms and vanished again in a blaze of three figures; but never possessed – until now. All was modest – O, so very modest! But all was my very own, and, what was more, everything in that room was exactly right.

After three or four visits, the uncanniness of the repetition set me thinking. Could it possibly be, that this was no dream at all? Had this chamber, perhaps, a real existence, and was I all the time leading, somewhere, another life – a life within a life – a life that I constantly forgot, within the life that I happened to remember? I tried my best to bring the thing to absolute proof. First, there was that frequent sense of extreme physical weariness with which I was wont to confront the inevitable up-rising of the morning – might not that afford a clue? Alas, no: I traced my mornings back, far behind the beginnings of the dream. I could not remember a day, since those rare white ones at school when it was a whole holiday, and summer was boon and young, when I had faced the problem of getting up with anything but a full sense of disgust. Next I thought, I will consult my accounts. Rooms must be paid for in London, however modest they may be; and the blessed figures can't lie. Then I recollected that I did not keep any accounts – never *had* kept any accounts – never intended to keep any beastly accounts – and, on the whole, I confess I was rather glad. Statistics would have been a mean prosaic way of plucking out the heart of this mystery. My only chance seemed to lie in coming across the place by accident. Then perhaps the extinguished torch would rekindle, the darkened garret of memory would be re-illumined, and it would be in my power at last to handle those rare editions, not capriciously as now, but at any hour I pleased. So I hunted Gray's Inn, Staple Inn, Clifford's Inn; hung about by-streets in Bloomsbury, even backwaters in Chelsea; but all to no result. It waits, that sequestered chamber, it waits for the serene moment when the brain is in just the apt condition, and ready to switch on the other memory even as one switches on the electric light with a turn of the wrist. Fantasy? well – perhaps. But the worst of it is, one never can feel quite sure. Only a dream, of course. And yet – the enchanting possibility!

And this possibility, which (one feels convinced) the wilful brain could make reality in a moment if it were only in the right humour, might be easily brought about by some accidental physical cause, some touch, scent, sound, gifted with the magic power of recall. Could my fingers but pass over the smooth surface of those oak balustrades so familiar to me, in a trice I would stand at the enchanted door. Could I even see in some casual shop-window one of those prints my other existence hoards so safe and sure – but that is unlikely indeed. Those prints of the dim land of dreams, ''they never are sold in the merchant's mart!'' Still, if one were only to turn up, in twopenny box or dusty portfolio, down in Southwark, off the roaring Strand, or somewhere along the quaint unclassified Brompton Road, in a flash the darkness would be day, the crooked would be made straight, and no policeman would be called upon to point out the joyous way.

If I have special faith in this sort of divining-rod, it is because of a certain strange case I once encountered and never quite elucidated. There was a certain man, respectable enough in every particular: wore drab spats all the year round, lived in a suburb, and did daily business on the ''Baltic''. When the weather was fine, and a halcyon calm brooded o'er the surface of the Baltic, instead of taking his suburban train at Cannon Street, he used to walk as far as Charing Cross: and before departing, if time allowed, he would turn into the National Gallery. Of a catholic mind, for he had never strayed down the tortuous byways of Art, he only went in to be amused, and was prepared to take his entertainment from all schools alike, without any of the narrow preferences of the cultured. From the very first, however, the Early Tuscans gripped him with a strange fascination, so that he rarely penetrated any further. What it was precisely that so detained him could never be ascertained. The man was not apt in the expression of subtle emotion, and never succeeded in defining the strong "possession" – for such it seemed to be – by which he was caught and held. The next phase in the case was, that he took to disappearing. He disappeared literally and absolutely – sometimes for a few days, sometimes for a fortnight or more; and on his return could tell nothing, explain nothing. Indeed, he did not seem to be really conscious of any absence. It was noted in time that his disappearances always coincided with his visits to the National Gallery. Thither he could be tracked; there all trace of him would cease. His female relations – an unimaginative, uneducated crew – surmised the unkindest things in their narrow way. Still, even they found it difficult to fling a stone at the Early Tuscans. For myself, I like to think that there was some bit of another life hidden away in him – some tranced memory of another far-away existence on Apennine slopes – which some quality in these pictures, and in these alone, had power to evoke. And I love to think that, transformed by this magic touch back into the other man of him, he passed, dream-possessed, forth from the portico, through Trafalgar Square, and into Charing Cross Station. That there, oblivious of all suburbs, he purchased one of those little books of coupons so much more romantic than your vulgar inland slip of pasteboard, and in due course sped Southwards – irresistibly drawn – took the Alps in a series of whorls, burrowings, and breathless flights o'er torrent and fall – till he basked at last, still speeding South, in the full sunlight that steeps the Lombard plain. Arrived in time, where his destiny (which was also his past) awaited him, I could see him, avoiding clamour of piazza, shunning prim airlessness of Galleria and Accademia, climbing the white road to where, in some little village or red-tiled convent, lurked the creation, madonna or saint, that held the other end of the subtle thread. The boy-lover, had he been, of this prim-tressed model? Or the St. George or

homely St. Roch who guarded her? Or himself the very painter?
Whatever the bond, here I could imagine him to linger, steeping
his soul in the picture and in the surroundings so native both to it
and to the man whose life for a brief minute he lived again, till
such time as that sullen devil within him – the later memory of
the man he also was – began to stir drowsily and to urge him
homewards, even as the other had urged him out. Once back, old
sights and sounds would develop the later man into full being and
consciousness, and as before he would tread the floor of the
Baltic, while oblivion swallowed the Tuscan existence – until the
next time!

These instances, it is true, are but "sports" in oblivion-lore.
But, putting aside such puzzle-fragments of memory, it is
impossible not to realize, in sad seriousness, that of all our
recollection has once held, by far the larger part must be by this
time in the realm of the forgotten; and that every day some fresh
delightful little entity pales, sickens, and passes over to the
majority. Sir Thomas Browne has quaintly written concerning
the first days of the young world, "when the living might exceed
the dead, and to depart this world could not be properly said, to
go unto the greater number"; but in these days of crowded
thought, of the mind cultured and sensitised to receive such a
swarm of impressions, no memory that sighs its life out but joins
a host far exceeding what it leaves behind. 'Tis but a scanty wallet
that each of us carries at his back. Few, indeed, and of a sorry
mintage, the thin coins that jingle therein. Our gold, lightly won,
has been as lightly scattered, along waysides left far behind.
Oblivion, slowly but surely stalking us, gathers it with a full arm,
and on the floor of his vast treasure-house stacks it in shining
piles.

And if it is the larger part that has passed from us, why not
also the better part? Indeed, logic almost requires it; for to select
and eliminate, to hold fast and let go at will, is not given to us. As
we jog along life's highroad, the knowledge of this inability dogs
each conscious enjoyment, till with every pleasant experience
comes also the annoying reflection, that it is a sheer toss-up
whether this is going to be a gain, a solid profit to carry along

with us, or fairy gold that shall turn to dust and nothingness in a few short mornings at best. As we realize our helplessness in the matter, we are almost ready to stamp and to swear. Will no one discover the chemical which shall fix the fleeting hue? That other recollection, now – that humiliating, that disgusting experience of ten years ago – *that* is safe enough, permanent, indestructible, warranted not to fade. If in this rag-fair we were only allowed to exchange and barter, to pick and choose! Oblivion, looking on, smiles grimly. It is he that shall select, not we; our part is but to look on helplessly, while – though he may condescend to leave us a pearl or two – the bulk of our jewels is swept into his pocket.

One hope alone remains to us, by way of consolation. These memories whose passing we lament, they are torpid only, not dead. They lie in a charmed sleep, whence a chance may awaken them, a touch make the dry bones live; though at present we know not the waking spell. Like Arthur, they have not perished, but only passed, and like him they may come again from the Avalon where they slumber. The chance is small, indeed. But the Merlin who controls these particular brain-cells, fitful and capricious though he be, after the manner of magicians, has powers to which we dare not assign limits. At any moment the stop may be pulled out, the switch pressed, the key turned, the Princess kissed. Then shall the spell-bound spring to life, the floodgates rise, the baked arid canals gleam with the silver tide; and once more we shall be fulfilled of the old joys, the old thrills, the old tears and laughter.

Better still – perhaps best of all – as those joyous old memories, hale and fresh once more, troop out of the catacombs into the light, these insistent ones of the present, this sullen host that beleaguers us day and night with such threatening obsession, may vanish, may pass, may flee away utterly, gone in their turn to lodge with Oblivion – and a good riddance!

6

"The Busy Little Population"

"Fastening their boat to a willow," writes Grahame in "The Piper at the Gates of Dawn", "the friends landed in this silent, silver kingdom, and patiently explored the hedges, the hollow trees, the tunnels and their little culverts, the ditches and dry water-ways." So begins one of the most intriguing episodes in *The Wind in the Willows*, culminating in the extraordinary encounter by Mole and Rat with the half-man, half-beast god called Pan.

For some critics, this experience takes us to the very heart of Kenneth Grahame's philosophy about wildlife, and certainly its mixture of fact and fantasy makes it quite unique. What is particularly striking about the chapter is its insight into the relationship between small animals and the forces of nature which control their destiny.

Grahame, as we know, had almost literally devoted his life to understanding the minds of wild creatures, their hopes and fears, their motivations and observances, and "The Piper at the Gates of Dawn" represents one of his most profound statements on what he has learned. It was the embodiment of what he had seen and heard over many years in the neighbourhood of Berkshire and Oxfordshire, as well as a distillation of what he had written in a number of earlier essays, in particular "The Inner Ear" and "The Lost Centaur".

"The Inner Ear" is a magical journey transporting the city-bound reader from the hurly-burly of his life into the quiet, still world of nature's small creatures, birds and animals alike. It conjures up vividly Grahame's days spent silently observing the

*The weir at Pangbourne. Local tradition claims that
Grahame used to sit writing in the boathouse
overlooking the river.*

"busy little population", as he calls these creatures, and developing his "inner ear" to understand the meaning of what they were doing. Like "The Iniquity of Oblivion", it was contributed to *The Yellow Book* of April 1895 and has never been reprinted.

"The Lost Centaur" is Grahame's first portrait of the Pan of *The Wind in the Willows*, and one of the earliest essays in which he expressed his very special attitude towards animals. In it he makes it quite clear that for him wild animals are morally equal, if not actually superior, to man. They are the ones we should be looking to as our teachers rather than forever believing we are their betters. Commenting on "The Lost Centaur" and another similar essay that Grahame wrote called "Orion" (included in his collection *Pagan Papers*), Peter Green has written:

"They both state, very clearly, the same thesis: that man has fatally neglected the instinctive, animal side of his nature through spiritual pride, puritan repression, and material greed; and that this neglect will take its toll in outbursts of neurotic irresponsibility. [Shades of Toad's adventures here!] In the first the symbol of unity is Cheiron, the wise Centaur, half man, half beast, and the emphasis is laid on the follies of unilateral development, the atrophy of the senses produced by over-emphasis on cold and rational logic. 'Orion' extends the metaphor: the celestial Hunter, the primitive element in mankind, is contrasted with the Children of the Plough, the miserable half-men produced by centuries of civilisation."

And Mr. Green is in no doubt about the importance of these two essays: "Safe in Victorian England, Grahame probably did not recognise what a powder-mine he had stumbled on. If in old age he had been told that these essays in ways anticipated both Freud and D. H. Lawrence he would have been frankly incredulous. Yet the truth is there: and at some point Grahame swerved away from its implications, retreated to a safe compromise, refused the challenge."

Even without such considerations, "The Lost Centaur" and "The Inner Ear" are for me particularly important stepping-stones to the understanding of Kenneth Grahame's mind, as well as of the way in which he constructed *The Wind in the Willows*.

They take us clear to the heart of the secret world of Mole, Rat, Badger and Toad, and underline still further what a unique vision was possessed by the creator of them all.

* * *

THE INNER EAR

TO all of us journeymen in this great whirling London mill, it happens sooner or later that the clatter and roar of its ceaseless wheels – a thing at first portentous, terrifying, nay, not to be endured – becomes a part of our nature, with our clothes and our acquaintances; till at last the racket and din of a competitive striving humanity not only cease to impinge on the sense, but induce a certain callosity in the organ, while that more sensitive inner ear of ours, once almost as quick to record as his in the fairy tale, who lay and heard the grass-blades thrust and sprout, from lack of exercise drops back to the rudimentary stage. Hence it comes about, that when we are set down for a brief Sunday, far from the central roar, our first sensation is that of a stillness corporeal, positive, aggressive. The clamorous ocean of sound has ebbed to an infinite distance; in its place this other sea of fullest silence comes crawling up, whelming and flooding us, its crystalline waves lapping us round with a possessing encircle-ment as distinct as that of the other angry tide now passed away and done with. The very Spirit of Silence is sitting hand in hand with us, and her touch is a real warm thing.

And yet, may not our confidence be premature? Even as we bathe and steep our senses refreshingly in this new element, that inner ear of ours begins to revive and to record, one by one, the real facts of sound. The rooks are the first to assert themselves. All this time that we took to be so void of voice they have been volubly discussing every detail of domestic tree-life, as they rock and sway beside their nests in the elm-tops. To take in the varied chatter of rookdom would in itself be a full morning's occupation, from which the most complacent might rise humble and instructed. Unfortunately, their talk rarely tends to edification.

The element of personality – the *argumentum ad hominem* –
always crops up so fatally soon, that long ere a syllogism has been
properly unrolled, the disputants have clinched on inadequate foot-
hold, and flopped thence, dishevelled, into space. Somewhere
hard by, their jackdaw cousins are narrating those smoking-room
stories they are so fond of, with bursts of sardonic laughter at the
close. For theology or the fine arts your jackdaw has little taste;
but give him something sporting and spicy, with a dash of the
divorce court, and no Sunday morning can ever seem too long.
At intervals the drum of the woodpecker rattles out from the
heart of a copse; while from every quarter birds are delivering
each his special message to the great cheery-faced postman who is
trudging his daily round overhead, carrying good tidings to the
whole bird-belt that encircles the globe. To all these wild, natural
calls of the wood, the farmyard behind us responds with its more
cultivated clamour and cackle; while the very atmosphere is
resonant of its airy population, each of them blowing his own
special trumpet. Silence, indeed! why, as the inner ear awakes
and develops, the solid bulk of this sound-in-stillness becomes in
its turn overpowering, terrifying. Let the development only
continue, one thinks, but a little longer, and the very rush of sap,
the thrust and foison of germination, will join in the din, and go
far to deafen us. One shrinks, in fancy, to a dwarf of meanest aims
and pettiest account before this army of full-blooded, shouting
soldiery, that possesses land and air so completely, with such an
entire indifference, too, towards ourselves, our conceits, and our
aspirations.

Here it is again, this lesson in modesty that nature is eternally
dinning into us; and the completeness of one's isolation in the
midst of all this sounding vitality cannot fail to strike home to the
most self-centred. Indeed, it is evident that we are entirely super-
fluous here; nothing has any need of us, nor cares to know what
we are interested in, nor what other people have been saying of
us, nor whether we go or stay. Those rooks up above have their
own society and occupations, and don't wish to share or impart
them; and if haply a rook seems but an insignificant sort of being
to you, be sure that you are quite as insignificant to the rook.

Nay, probably more so; for while you at least allot the rook his special small niche in creation, it is more than doubtful whether he ever troubles to ''place'' you at all. He has weightier matters to occupy him, and so long as you refrain from active interference, the chances are that for him you simply don't exist.

But putting birds aside, as generally betraying in their startled, side-glancing mien some consciousness of a featherless unaccountable tribe that may have to be reckoned with at any moment, those other winged ones, the bees and their myriad cousins, simply insult one at every turn with their bourgeois narrowness of non-recognition. Nothing, indeed, could be more unlike the wary watchful marches of the bird-folk than the bustling self-centred devotion to business of these tiny brokers in Nature's busy mart. If you happen to get in their way, they jostle up against you, and serve you right; if you keep clear of the course, they proceed serenely without so much as a critical glance at your hat or your boots. Snubbed, hustled, and ignored, you feel, as you retire from the unequal contest, that the scurrying alarm of bird or beast is less hurtful to your self-respect than this complacent refusal of the insect to admit your very existence.

In sooth, we are at best poor fusionless incapable bodies; unstable of purpose, veering betwixt hot fits and chill, doubtful at times whether we have any business here at all. The least we can do is to make ourselves as small as possible, and interfere as little as may be with these lusty citizens, knowing just what they want to do, and doing it, at full work in a satisfactory world that is emphatically theirs, not ours.

The more one considers it, the humbler one gets. This pleasant, many-hued, fresh-smelling world of ours would be every whit as goodly and fair, were it to be rid at one stroke of us awkward aliens, staggering pilgrims through a land whose customs and courtesies we never entirely master, whose pleasant places we embellish and sweeten not at all. We, on the other hand, would be bereft indeed, were we to wake up one chill morning and find that all these practical capable cousins of ours had packed up and quitted in disgust, tired of trying to assimilate us, weary of our aimlessness, our brutalities, our ignorance of real life.

Our dull inner ear is at last fully awake, fully occupied. It must be a full three hundred yards away, that first brood of ducklings, fluffily proud of a three-days-old past; yet its shrill peep-peep reaches us as distinctly as the worry-worry of bees in the peach-blossom a foot from our head. Then suddenly – the clank of a stable-bucket on the tiles, the awakening of church-bells – humanity, with its grosser noises, is with us once more, and at the first sound of it, affrighted, the multitudinous drone of the under-life recedes, ebbs, vanishes; Silence, the nymph so shy and withdrawn, is by our side again, and slips her hand into ours.

*   *   *

THE LOST CENTAUR

OF strange and divers strands is twisted the mysterious cord that, reaching back "through spaces out of space and timeless time", somewhere joins us to the Brute; a twine of mingled yarn, not utterly base, As we grow from our animal infancy, and the threads snap one by one at each gallant wing-stroke of a soul poising for flight into Empyrean, we are yet conscious of a loss for every gain, we have some forlorn sense of a vanished heritage. Willing enough are we to "let the ape and tiger die"; but the pleasant cousins dissembled in hide and fur and feather are not all tigers and apes: which last vile folk, indeed, exist for us only in picture-books, and chiefly offend by always carrying the Sunday School ensign of a Moral at their tails. Others – happily of less didactic dispositions – there be; and it is to these unaffected, careless companions that the sensible child is wont to devote himself; leaving severely alone the stiff, tame creatures claiming to be of closer kin. And yet these playmates, while cheerfully admitting him of their fellowship, make him feel his inferiority at every point. Vainly, his snub nose projected earthwards, he essays to sniff it with the terrier who (as becomes the nobler animal) is leading in the chase; and he is ready to weep as he realises his loss. And the rest of the Free Company, – the pony, the cows, the great cart-horses, – are ever shaming him by their unboastful exercise of some enviable and unattainable attribute. Even the friendly pig, who (did but parents permit) should eat of his bread and drink of his cup, and be unto him as a brother, – which among all these unhappy forked radishes, so cheery, so unambitious, so purely contented, so apt to be the guide, philosopher, and friend of boyhood as he? What wonder that at times, when the neophyte in life begins to realise that all these desirable accomplishments have had to be surrendered one by one in the process of developing a Mind, the course of fitting out a Lord of Creation, he is wont – not knowing the extent of the kingdom to which he is heir – to feel a little discontented?

Ere now this ill-humour, taking root in a nature wherein the animal is already ascendant, has led by downward paths to the Goat-Foot in whom the submerged human system, peeps out but fitfully, at exalted moments. He, the peevish and irascible, shy of trodden ways and pretty domesticities, is linked to us by little but his love of melody; but for which saving grace, the hair would soon creep up from thigh to horn of him. At times he will still do us a friendly turn: will lend a helping hand to poor little Psyche, wilfully seeking her own salvation; will stand shoulder to shoulder with us on Marathon plain. But in the main his sympathies are first for the Beast: to which his horns are never horrific, but his hairy pelt is ever natural and familiar, his voice (with its talk of help and healing) not harsh nor dissonant but voice of very brother as well as very god. And this declension – for declension it is, though we achieve all the confidences of Melampus, and even master his pleasant slang – may still be ours if we suffer what lives in us of our primal cousins to draw us down. And let soul inform and irradiate body as it may, the threads are utterly shorn asunder never: nor is man, the complete, the self-contained, permitted to cut himself wholly adrift from these his poor relations. The mute and stunted human embryo that gazes appealingly from out the depths of their eyes must ever remind him of a kinship once (possibly) closer. Nay, at times, it must even seem to whelm him in reproach. As thus: "Was it really necessary, after all, that we two should part company so early? May you not have taken a wrong turning somewhere, in your long race after your so-called progress, after the perfection of this be-lauded species of yours? A turning whose due avoidance might perhaps have resulted in no such lamentable cleavage as is here, but in some perfect embodiment of the dual nature: as who should say a being with the nobilities of both of us, the basenesses of neither? So might you, more fortunately guided, have been led at last up the green sides of Pelion, to the ancestral, the primeval, Centaur still waiting majestic on the summit!'' It is even so. Perhaps this thing might once have been, O cousin outcast and estranged! But the opportunity was long since lost. Henceforth, two ways for us for ever!

7

"The Call of the South"

"Wayfarers All" has been described as the most quoted chapter of all in *The Wind in the Willows*. Certainly, it is unlike any other in the book, taking the reader far from the confines of the River Bank and the Wild Wood, on a journey south in search of the sun and new horizons. Although the trip is accomplished simply through the storytelling of the Sea Rat, it is so vividly described, so engrossing and colourful, that it must surely be based on the author's own experiences. And so it proves.

The patient listener, Rat, is, however, very much at the heart of the chapter, first conversing with a group of swallows who tell him of their annual compulsion to head south. "We feel it stirring within us, a sweet unrest," says one, "then back come the recollections, one by one, like homing pigeons. They flutter through our dreams at night, they fly with us in our wheelings and circlings by day." And another adds dreamily, "Ah, yes, the call of the South, of the South! Its songs, its hues, its radiant air! O, do you remember——"

Then, with these words still ringing in his ears, Rat meets the "lean and keen-featured wayfarer" in his faded blue jersey and patched and stained breeches – the Sea Rat. He, too, takes up the same theme as the birds. "Here am I," he says, "footsore and hungry, tramping southward, following the old call, back to the old life, the life which is mine and which will not let me go."

The traveller tells the entranced Rat how he left his comfortable little upland farm to follow the call, and about the adventures on land and sea that have since befallen him. And "the Water Rat, silent and enthralled, floated on dream-canals and

*Fowey, Cornwall, where the Grahames spent many
summer holidays – the origin of the Sea Rat's "little
grey sea town that clings along one steep side of the
harbour".*

heard a phantom song pealing high between vaporous grey wave-lapped walls.'' In the end, it is only the resolution of the home-loving Mole that forcibly prevents his friend from following this spellbinding figure when he sets off on his travels once more.

Despite his devotion to the rural heart of England, Kenneth Grahame also adored travelling, and during the course of his life made frequent trips to the sunny countries of the south – Italy, in particular – which he eulogises in this chapter. The sea also fascinated him, and he spent many a holiday with friends at the Cornish port of Fowey – the ''little grey sea town that clings along one steep side of the harbour'' as the Sea Rat lyrically describes it. It was here, too, that Grahame found the inspiration for the character of the Sea Rat.

We find the clue to this in a letter he wrote to a friend from Fowey in 1899. ''My sister said that she went along the cliffs and climbed down to a little cove and as she sat there a big rat came out and sat beside her and ate winkles!'' Grahame writes. ''Said I to my sister, 'Did he buy them off a barrow and drop them into his hat?' But she looked puzzled and said, 'No, he only scraped in the seaweed with his little paws and fetched them out.' Then I began again – 'Was it a *black* pin that he ate them with?' And she thought I was raving so I dropped the subject. But had *I* been there he'd have given me winkles and I'd have lent him a pin out of my tie.'' Thus does the Sea Rat make his first appearance nine years before his bewitching performance in *The Wind in the Willows*.

When Kenneth Grahame came to write ''Wayfarers All'' there were not only his memories of Cornwall and the warmer climes of Italy to inspire him, but also at least two essays he had penned earlier. ''The Wayfarer'', which was part of a con-tribution to *The Yellow Book* in July 1895, perfectly expresses the ''sweet unrest'' in his own mind, and in the ''bare-legged man'' he meets, formerly ''the Secretary to some venerable Company'', who tells him of his voyaging southwards, there is the human counterpart of the Sea Rat for all to see. This piece, with Grahame playing Rat as he listens to the tales of his new-found companion, is an almost identical rehearsal for ''Wayfarers

All''. Reading it in the knowledge of the longings that must have been pulling at Grahame, it is remarkable that he was ever able to drag himself back to his job at the Bank of England!

The second essay, "The Triton's Conch", which he contributed to the *National Observer* in December 1893, emphasises his love affair with the sea, and was evidently inspired by one of his trips to Fowey. Here, too, one can hear the voice that, in the episode of "Wayfarers All", reveals such love of the mysterious places on the edge of experience.

* * *

THE WAYFARER

WORN and depressed by harrying troubles I dreamt that I sped south over the sea, to a sunny isle far South in the Atlantic. There, existing many days in the balmy present, alone, new life and strength flowed silently in with every minute of warmth and peace. Till it happened, one odorous night, that I sat watching the large Southern stars while the ocean chimed with lazy rise and fall in the bay below. Then first, and suddenly, my thoughts flew back to the far-away northern island, arena of strife and all the crowd of petty vexations. Now, how small they all seemed! How simple the unravelling of the baffling knots! How orderly and easy the way to meet them and brush them by! So that I, sitting there in the South, seemed to be saying to my struggling self in the North, "If I were you, how easily would I make my way through these petty obstacles! and how helpless and incapable you are in a little strait!" And myself in the North, put on defence, and seemed to reply: "And if I were you, so would I – with your fuller knowledge, fuller strength. As it is, perhaps on the whole I do my best." And myself in the South, in justice forced to assent, returned, "Well yes, perhaps after all you do your best – a sorry best, but as much as can fairly be expected of you." Then I woke, startled at the point to which my dream had led me.

Will it be just like this again? Sitting one day on the dim eternal shore, shall I look back, see and pity my past poor human strivings? And say then, as now, ''Well, perhaps, little cripple, you did your best, a sorry one though, you poor little, handicapped, human soul''?

Some there are who have the rare courage, at the realising point, to kick the board over and declare against further play. Stout-hearted ones they, worthy of marble and brass; but you meet them not at every turn of the way. Such a man I forgathered with by accident, one late autumn, on the almost deserted Lido. The bathing-ladders were drawn up, the tramway was under repair; but the slant sun was still hot on the crinkled sand, and it was not so much a case of paddling suggesting itself as of finding oneself barefoot and paddling without any conscious process of thought. So I paddled along dreamily, and thought of Ulysses, and how he might have run the prow of his galley up on these very sands, and sprung ashore and paddled; and then it was that I met him – not Ulysses, but the instance in point.

He was barelegged also, this elderly man of sixty or thereabouts; and he had just found a *cavallo del mare*, and exhibited it with all the delight of a boy; and as we wandered together, cool-footed, eastwards, I learnt by degrees how such a man as this, with the mark of Cheapside still evident on him, came to be pacing the sands of the Lido that evening with me. He had been Secretary, it transpired, to some venerable Company or Corporation that dated from Henry VII; and among his duties, which were various and engrossing, was in especial that of ticking off, with a blue pencil, the members of his governing body, as they made their appearance at their weekly meeting; in accordance with the practice dating from Henry VII. His week, as I have said, was a busy one, and hinged on a Board day; and as time went on these Board days raced up and disappeared with an ever-increasing rapidity, till at last his life seemed to consist of but fifty-two days in the year – all Board days. And eternally he seemed to be ticking off names with a feverish blue pencil. These names, too, that he ticked – they flashed into sight and vanished with the same nightmare gallop; the whole business was a great humming zoetrope. Anon the Board would consist of Smith, Brown, Jackson, &c., Life Members all; in the briefest of spaces Smith would drop out, and on would come Price, a neophyte – a mere youngling, this Price. A few more Board days flashed by, and out would go Brown and maybe Jackson – on would come Cattermole, Fraser, Davidson – beardless juniors every one. Round spun the unceasing wheel; in a twinkling Davidson, the fledgling, sat reverend in the chair, while as for those others –! And all the time his blue pencil, with him, its slave, fastened to one end of it, ticked steadily on. To me, the hearer, it was evident that he must have been gradually getting into the same state of mind as Rudyard Kipling's delightful lighthouse keeper, whom solitude and the ceaseless tides caused to see streaks and lines in all things, till at last he barred a waterway of the world against the ships that persisted in making the water streaky. And this may account for an experience of his in the Underground Railway one evening, when he was travelling home after a painful Board day on which he had ticked up three new boys into vacant places which seemed to have been hardly filled an hour. He was alone, he said, and rather sleepy, and he hardly looked at the stranger who got in at one of the stations, until he saw him deposit in the hat-rack – where ordinary people put their umbrellas – what might have been an umbrella, but looked, in the dim light of the Underground, far more like a scythe. Then he sat up and began to take notice. The elderly stranger – for he was both gaunt and elderly – nay, as he looked at him longer he saw that he was old – oh, so very old! And one long white tuft of hair hung down on his wrinkled forehead from under his top hat, – the stranger squatted on the seat opposite him, produced a note-book and a pencil – a *blue* pencil too! – and leaning forward, with a fiendish grin, said, "*Now* I'm going to tick off all you fellows – all you Secretaries – right back from the days of Henry the Seventh!"

The Secretary fell back helplessly in his seat. Terror-stricken, he strove to close his ears against the raucous voice that was already rattling off those quaint old Tudor names he remembered having read on yellowing parchment; but all was of no avail. The stranger went steadily on, and each name as read was ruthlessly scored out by the unerring blue pencil. The pace was tremendous. Already they were in the Commonwealth; past flew the Restoration like a racehorse – the blue pencil wagged steadily like a nightmare – Queen Anne and her coffee-houses – in a second they were left far behind; and as they turned the corner and sped down the straight of the Georgian era, the Secretary sweated, a doomed man. The gracious reign of Victoria was full in sight – nay, on the stranger's lips was hovering the very name of Fladgate – Fladgate whom the Secretary could himself just remember, a doddering old pensioner – when the train shivered and squealed into St. James's Park Station. The Secretary flung the door open and fled like a hare, though it was not his right station. He ran as far as the Park itself, and there on the bridge over the water he halted, mopped his brow, and gradually recovered his peace of mind. The evening was pleasant, full of light and laughter and the sound of distant barrel-organs. Before him, calm and cool, rose the walls of the India Office, which in his simple way he had always considered a dream in stone. Beneath his feet a whole family of ducks circled aimlessly, with content written on every feature; or else, reversing themselves in a position denoting supreme contempt for all humanity above the surface, explored a new cool underworld a few inches below. It was then (he said) that a true sense of his situation began to steal over him; and it was then that he awoke to the fact of another life open to him should he choose to grasp it. Neither the ducks nor the India Office (so he affirmed) carried blue pencils, and why should he? The very next Board day he sent in his resignation, and, with a comfortable pension and some reminiscence (perhaps) of that frontage of the India Office, crossed the Channel and worked South till he came to Venice, where the last trace of blue-pencil nightmare finally faded away.

"And are you never bored?" I tenderly inquired of him, as we rocked homewards in a gondola between an apricot sky and an apricot sea.

"During the first six months I was," he answered, frankly; "then it passed away altogether, even as influenza does in time, or the memory of a *gaucherie*. And now every day lasts as long as a year of those Board days of old, and is fifty-two times as interesting. Why, only take this afternoon, for example. I didn't get over here till two, but first I met some newly-arrived Americans, and talked for a cycle with them; and you never know what an American will be surprised at, or, better still, what he will not be surprised at; and if you only think what that means— Well, presently they left (they had to get on to Rome), so I went up to the platform over the sea and had oysters and a bottle of that delightful yellow wine I always forget the name of; and aeons passed away in the consumption. Each oyster lasted a whole Board day, and each glass of yellow wine three. Then I strolled along the sands for a century or so, thinking of nothing in particular. Lastly, I met you, and for some twelve months I've been boring you with my uninteresting story. And even yet there's the whole evening to come! Oh, I had lots of leeway to make up when I came over here; but I think I shall manage it yet – in Venice!''

I could not help thinking, as I parted from him at the Piazzetta steps, that (despite a certain incident in the Underground Railway) here was one of the sanest creatures I had ever yet happened upon.

But examples such as this (as I said) are rare; the happy-starred ones who know when to cut their losses. The most of us prefer to fight on – mainly, perhaps, from cowardice, and the dread of a plunge into a new element, new conditions, new surroundings – a fiery trial for any humble, mistrustful creature of use-and-wont. And yet it is not all merely a matter of funk. For a grim love grows up for the sword-play itself, for the push and the hurtle of battle, for the grips and the give-and-take – in fine, for the fight itself, whatever the cause. In this exhaltation, far from ignoble, we push and worry along until a certain day of a mist and a choke, and we are ticked off and done with.

This is the better way; and the history of our race is ready to justify us. With the tooth-and-claw business we began, and we mastered it thoroughly ere we learnt any other trade. Since that time we may have achieved a thing or two besides – evolved an art, even, here and there, though the most of us bungled it. But from first to last fighting was the art we were always handiest at;

and we are generally safe if we stick to it, whatever the foe, whatever the weapons – most of all, whatever the cause.

* * *

THE TRITON'S CONCH

FROM each generation certain are chosen whom Nature, in those rathe years when she imprints our plastic wax with that wonderful signet-ring of hers, leads by the hand one fated day within sight and sound of the sea. There – howbeit scarce in years enough to distinguish between vision and fact – the elect is made aware, or dreams, of a marvellous emergence and dazedly hears the very Triton blow on his wreathed horn. And in the blare that issues from out the crooks of the sea-thing's shell are mingled many elements – wind-shaken water, whip and creak and rattle of shrouds, flap of idle sails in halcyon spells, cry of gulls at pasture on the pale acres that know no plough; but run through them all, making the chord perfect, is a something that suggests the dazzling laughter of Oceanus in a crinkling calm, with a certain haunting smell of weed and tar. Henceforth, that adept is possessed. Deskbound, pent in between city walls – a fellow, say, fast held in the tangle of Christ Church bells; a solicitor behind wire-blinds in some inland market-town – henceforth the insistent echo will awake and take him betimes, claiming him as one with the trident brand on him. For the Triton knows his man, and whom he has once chosen he never again lets go.

This thing may befall him, indeed, who has never even sniffed salt in the air, nor watched the solan, a rocket reversed, spirt high the spray in his joyous huntings. On him it will come suddenly out of some musty book of magic: wherein the sulphur clouds roll tremendous round the tall masts of fighting ships topped by the meteor flag, or the boats, with muffled oars, steal forth to the cutting out of the French brig. He will hear the lap and gurgle of waves he has never seen, along the sides of a craft whose streaks no man has laid: wherefore it has come to pass that many a stout mariner of England has known nothing more nautical than the brown sails of barges sliding by his farmstead, through pasturage dotted with browsing kine. If the conditions be reversed, and Nature, as first known to him, was ever one half of it the shifting sea, then the Triton will have certainly hailed him one day or other, and thenceforward the call sounds ever in his ear. Or, it may be, having thrilled to the Triton's note ere he knew right from wrong, the vision it evokes for him shall be circumscribed and homely as the writer's own: which is of big black-sided fishing-boats, drawn high and dry on a wondrous beach. These were his daily food, though once a week the mysterious steamer from the outer world crawled by with clockwork singularity. Fishing-boats and the weekly steamer – these he had endlessly limned and dislimned, though the slate was given (sure) for better ends, ere the white day when the little plump of yachts cast anchor off the tiny town. The first reading of the *Arabian Nights* – they were something like that to him, these slim Sultanas of the sea! Had not the rural policeman been courting his nursemaid, the vision had lacked completeness; to the young god he owes it, that he was rowed out, enraptured, himself and the maiden in the stern, the man of order at the oars, while the unseen Eros balanced it in the bows. The writhing golden sea-weed shimmered fathoms deep below. Above were these fairy galleys, and you could spy their dainty fitments, and spell out the names on their gilded bows. And when at last they spread white wings and vanished, the slate for long would record no meaner portraiture. It is small wonder that to this boy the trains whose acquaintance he was soon to make, should seem ungainly rattletraps. True it is that they held one piece of fascination; for the arms of an ancient city were painted on the carriage-doors, and these were made additionally mysterious by the rhyme communicated by a good-natured porter, which told how ''This is the tree that never grew, this is the bird that never flew; this is the fish that never swam, this is the bell that never rang.'' But for all that, the train was damned, in that it took you away, out of earshot of the Triton's bugling; so that only once you might get a certain small effect of grace when suddenly, as it rattled past some dingy town, over the reeking house-tops there appeared a tangled tracery of masts, while a delicate waft of tar and harbour-mud breathed of the authentic, unsuspected Paradise at hand.

Isled in far-reaching downs, the inland farmstead knows no harsh Atlantic: the sole murmur that surges and breaks about its doors commingles the cackle and grunt and lot of its dependants. Two china dogs of seductive aspect adorn the mantelshelf in a kitchen recking not of nets nor crab-pots, with certain fruits in wax, cunningly fashioned, fairer far than Nature's own, and with two great smooth shells, wherein the sea's secret lingers, in shadow as it were, and eternized. Once, long years ago, they were filled with the Triton's music, and ever since, the natural phonographs of the god, they have faithfully retained its echoes till the understanding one shall come. And as he listens at the lips of them, farm and farmstead melt away; the solid miles break up and disappear; and once again he is walking the wind-blown sands, while at his side his ancient mistress, malicious, serpentine, beautiful, coils and fawns, and laughs and caresses, and calls to him, as of old.

And what of the Triton's point of view? He, too, is doubtless drawn to an alien element by some subtle attraction not in the unstable glancing world wherein he abides. Is there far down in him a sympathetic string responding to the voice of the wind in the pine tops, the flow of gorse and heather, the hum of wandering bees? Hath he an affection for the warm-skinned beasts that stray by the shores, which the cold flocks and herds of Proteus fail to satisfy? Or doth he turn, perchance, from the chill caresses of green-haired mermaidens, to dream of some rich-blooded minion of the dairy? Whatever the reason, who doubts that there are discontents down in the sea as well as high on his banks? And neither of us can change places, which is possibly just as well. No: we can but hail each other fraternally, on those rare occasions when recognition is permitted, and the last tripper has left the beach one moment free.

8

" *The Hour of Toad* "

The conceited, headstrong, and irresponsible Toad, who first comes fully to our attention in the second chapter of the *The Wind in the Willows* and appears thereafter at regular intervals as the sorry catalogue of his adventures unfolds, is perhaps the best known of all the characters in the book. By some critics it has been suggested that he is modelled on Oscar Wilde, whom Grahame knew through his associations with *The Yellow Book*, and that Toad's misfortunes are actually that unfortunate man's experiences ''transmuted and scaled down to animal fantasy''. Others have detected in him something of the character of the notorious Horatio Bottomley, while a third group believes him to be a composite figure representing the landed gentry of the time, who squandered their money in feckless pursuits instead of working to preserve the rural environment which was their heritage.

Like all great works of literature, the text of *The Wind in the Willows* has attracted its fair share of analysis and search for hidden meanings. What remains incontrovertible is that the adventures of Toad were the first parts of the book devised by Kenneth Grahame, as a story for his son, and though he may have consciously or unconsciously grafted other elements into the character of Toad, when he actually came to write the story down on paper, Toad was in the first instance little more than ''a bad low animal''. I think that when we have waded through all the arguments, Peter Green is closest to the truth when he states:

''Grahame's attitude to Toad is extremely ambivalent. He is ostensibly on the side of the angels, yet shows very little sympathy for Authority as such. While condemning Toad's excesses, he has, one suspects, a sneaking urge to behave in exactly the same way: Toad, in fact, is a sublimation of all his own unrecognised desires, and is harried by the forces which Grahame himself found particularly terrifying. There is no one so congenitally scared of a magistrate as your thoroughgoing Bohemian: he has nightmares about prisons, pursuit, disgrace, the ineluctable hand of the law." Mr. Green adds that this pursuit-motive is repeated again and again in Toad's adventures, "most strikingly, perhaps, in the railway chase." Two early articles which I have uncovered give vivid expression to these thoughts and can be seen to have been influential in the development of Toad both in the early episodes as well as more particularly in chapters eight ("Toad's Adventures") and ten ("The Further Adventures of Toad").

Grahame's conflict within himself about the restrictions of society – the very rules that he makes Toad ignore or overthrow – are to be found expressed in "The Eternal Whither" which he wrote in July 1892 for the *National Observer*. Once again he takes the example of a City man who throws over the traces and heads off for a life of self-indulgence, with even the suggestion of falling prey to temptation. The fun to be had joy-riding in cars is given expression, as is the excitement of driving a locomotive – Toad's two consuming passions in the book. Here, indeed, are the seeds of that irrepressible animal's adventures!

"The Eternal Whither" is also intriguing for its reference to a lock-keeper. No reader will need reminding of Otter's "good story about Toad and the lock-keeper" which he leaves so tantalisingly unfinished. When Kenneth Grahame was still alive, one reader tried to drag out of him the truth of the matter, but he remained implacable. "I am afraid," he replied to his correspondent in 1923, "I must not tell you the story about Toad and the Lock-keeper. The fact is, they both lost their tempers, and said things they much regretted afterwards. They are now friends again, so we have all agreed to let the matter drop." Could it, I wonder, have been a little matter of unrequited love expressed by Toad to the waterman's daughter that caused the fuss? What a

The railway bridge over the Thames near Streatley,
where Grahame may have watched trains passing on
their way to Didcot and Oxford.

thought, you may say – but read ''The Eternal Whither'' and
you will see what I mean . . .

The other piece, ''The Romance of the Rail'' expresses
Grahame's love of the railway, a perhaps surprising fact for a man
who was so devoted to rural tranquillity. The essay was written
for the *National Observer* of August 1891, but is mainly based
on a journey he made from Scotland to London while he was still
a child. He gives a vivid impression of train travel, and much of

its atmosphere and rhythm is to be found transposed into Toad's madcap rail journey with the officers of the law hard on his heels.

* * *

THE ETERNAL WHITHER

THERE was once an old cashier in some ancient City establishment, whose practice was to spend his yearly holiday in relieving some turnpike-man at his post, and performing all the duties appertaining thereunto. This was vulgarly taken to be an instance of mere mill-horse enslavement to his groove – the reception of payments; and it was spoken of both in mockery of all mill-horses and for the due admonishment of others. And yet that clerk had discovered for himself an unique method of seeing Life at its best, the flowing, hurrying, travelling, marketing Life of the Highway; the life of bagman and cart, of tinker, and pig-dealer, and all cheery creatures that drink and chaffer together in the sun. He belonged, above all, to the scanty class of clear-seeing persons who know both what they are good for and what they really want. To know what you would like to do is one thing; to go out boldly and do it is another – and a rarer; and the sterile fields about Hell-Gate are strewn with the corpses of those who would if they could.

To be sure, being bent on the relaxation most congenial to one's soul, it is possible to push one's disregard for convention too far: as is seen in the case of another, though of an earlier generation, in the same establishment. In his office there was the customary ''attendance-book'', wherein the clerks were expected to sign each day. Here his name one morning ceases abruptly from appearing; he signs, indeed, no more. Instead of signature you find, a little later, writ in careful commercial hand, this entry: ''Mr. —— did not attend at his office today, having been hanged at eight o'clock in the morning for horse-stealing.'' Through the faded ink of this record do you not seem to catch, across the gulf of years, some waft of the jolly humanity which breathed in this prince among clerks? A formal precisian, doubtless, during business hours; but with just this honest love of horseflesh lurking deep down there in him – unsuspected, sweetening the whole lump. Can you not behold him, freed from his desk, turning to pursue his natural bent, as a city-bred dog still striveth to bury his bone deep in the hearth-rug? For no filthy lucre, you may be sure, but from sheer love of the pursuit itself! All the same, he erred; erred, if not in taste, at least in judgment: for we cannot entirely acquit him of blame for letting himself be caught.

In these tame and tedious days of the policeman rampant, our melancholy selves are debarred from many a sport, joyous and debonair, whereof our happier fathers were free. Book-stealing, to be sure, remains to us; but every one is not a collector; and, besides, 'tis a diversion you can follow with equal success all the year round. Still, the instance may haply be pregnant with suggestion to many who wearily ask each year, what new place or pursuit exhausted earth still keeps for the holiday-maker. 'Tis a sad but sober fact, that the most of men lead flat and virtuous lives, departing annually with their family to some flat and virtuous place, there to disport themselves in a manner that is decent, orderly, wholly uninteresting, vacant of every buxom stimulus. To such as these a suggestion, in all friendliness: why not try crime? We shall not attempt to specify the particular branch – for every one must himself seek out and find the path his nature best fits him to follow; but the general charm of the prospect must be evident to all. The freshness and novelty of secrecy, the artistic satisfaction in doing the act of self-expression as well as it can possibly be done; the experience of being not the hunter, but the hunted, not the sportsman, but the game; the delight of comparing and discussing crimes with your mates over a quiet pipe on your return to town; these new pleasures – these and their like – would furnish just that gentle stimulant, that peaceful sense of change so necessary to the tired worker. And then the fact, that you would naturally have to select and plan out your particular line of diversion without advice or assistance, has its own advantage. For the moment a man takes to dinning in your ears that you ought, you really ought, to go to Norway, you at once begin to hate Norway with a hate that ever will be; and to have Newlyn, Cromer, or Dawlish, Carinthia or the Austrian Tyrol jammed down your throat, is enough to initiate the discovery that your own individual weakness is a joyous and persistent liking for manslaughter.

Some few seem to be born without much innate tendency to crime. After all, it is mostly a matter of heredity; these unfortunates are less culpable than their neglectful ancesters; and it is a fault that none need really blush for in the present. For such as they there still remains the example of the turnpike-loving clerk, with all its golden possibilities. Denied the great delight of driving a locomotive, or a fire-engine – whirled along in a glorious nimbus of smoke-pant, spark-shower, and hoarse warning roar – what bliss to the palefaced quilldriver to command a penny steam-boat between London Bridge and Chelsea! to drive a four-horsed Jersey-car to Kew at sixpence a head! Though turnpikes be things of the past, there are still tolls to be taken on many a pleasant reach of Thames. What happiness in quiet moments to tend the lock-keeper's flowerbeds – perhaps make love to his daughter; anon in busier times to let the old gates swing, work the groaning winches, and hear the water lap and suck and gurgle as it slowly sinks or rises with its swaying freight; to dangle legs over the side and greet old acquaintances here and there among the parti-coloured wayfarers passing up or down; while tobacco palleth not on the longest day, and beer is ever within easy reach. The iron tetter that scurfs the face of our island has killed out the pleasant life of the road; but many of its best conditions still linger round these old toll-gates, free from dust and clatter, on the silent liquid Highway to the West.

These for the weaker brethren: but for him who is conscious of the Gift, the path is plain.

* * *

THE ROMANCE OF THE RAIL

IN these iron days of the dominance of steam, the crowning wrong that is wrought us of furnace and piston-rod lies in their annihilation of the steadfast mystery of the horizon, so that the imagination no longer begins to work at the point where vision ceases. In happier times, three hundred years ago, the sea-farers from Bristol City looked out from the prows of their vessels in the grey of the morning, and wot not rightly whether the land they saw might be Jerusalem or Madagascar, or if it were not North and South America. "And there be certaine flitting islands," says one, "which have been oftentimes seene, and when men approached near them they vanished." "It may be that the gulfs will wash us down," said Ulysses (thinking of what

Americans call the "getting-off place"); "it may be we shall touch the Happy Isles." And so on, and so on; each with his special hope or "wild surmise." There was always a chance of touching the Happy Isles. And in that first fair world whose men and manners we knew through story-books, before experience taught us far other, the Prince mounts his horse one fine morning, and rides all day, and sleeps in a forest; and next morning, lo! a new country: and he rides by fields and granges never visited before, through faces strange to him, to where an unknown King steps down to welcome the mysterious stranger. And he marries the Princess, and dwells content for many a year; till one day he thinks "I will look upon my father's face again, though the leagues be long to my own land." And he rides all day, and sleeps in a forest; and next morning he is made welcome at home, where his name has become a dim memory. Which is all as it should be; for, annihilate time and space as you may, a man's stride remains the true standard of distance; an eternal and unalterable scale. The severe horizon, too, repels the thoughts as you gaze to the infinite considerations that lie about, within touch and hail; and the night cometh, when no man can work.

To all these natural bounds and limitations it is good to get back now and again, from a life assisted and smooth by artificialities. Where iron has superseded muscle, the kindly life-blood is apt to throb dull as the measured beat of the steam-engine. But the getting back to them is now a matter of effort, of set purpose, a stepping aside out of our ordinary course; they are no longer unsought influences towards the making of character. So perhaps the time of them has gone by, here in this second generation of steam. *Pereunt et imputantur;* they pass away, and are scored against not us but our guilty fathers. For ourselves, our particular slate is probably filling fast. The romance of the steam-engine is yet to be captured and expressed – not fully nor worthily, perhaps, until it too is a vanished regret; though Emerson for one will not have it so, and maintains and justifies its right to immediate recognition as poetic material. "For as it is dislocation and detachment from the life of God that makes things ugly, the poet, who re-attaches things to Nature and the whole – re-attaching even artificial things and violations of Nature to Nature by a deeper insight – disposes very easily of the most disagreeable facts''; so that he looks upon ''the factory village and the railway'' and ''sees them fall within the great Order not less than the bee-hive or the spider's geometrical web.'' The poet, however, seems hard to convince hereof. Emerson will have it that ''Nature loves the gliding train of cars''; ''instead of which'' the poet still goes about the country singing purling brooks. Painters have been more flexible and liberal. Turner saw and did his best to seize the spirit of the thing, its kinship with the elements, and to blend furnace-glare and rush of iron with the storm shower, the wind and the thwart-flashing sun-rays, and to make the whole a single expression of irresoluble force. And even in a certain work by another and a very different painter – though I willingly acquit Mr. Frith of any deliberate romantic intention – you shall find the element of romance in the vestiges of the old order still lingering in the first transition period: the coach-shaped railway carriages with luggage piled and corded on top, the red-coated guard, the little engine tethered well ahead as if between traces. To those bred within sight of the sea, steamers will always partake in somewhat of the ''beauty and mystery of the ships''; above all, if their happy childhood have lain among the gleaming lochs and sinuous firths of the Western Highlands, where, twice a week maybe, the strange visitant crept by headland and bay, a piece of the busy, mysterious outer world. For myself, I probably stand alone in owning to a sentimental weakness for the night-piercing whistle – judiciously remote, as some men love the skirl of the pipes. In the days when streets were less wearily familiar than now, or ever the golden cord was quite loosed that led back to relinquished fields and wider skies, I have lain awake on stifling summer nights, thinking of luckier friends by moor and stream, and listening for the whistles from certain railway stations, veritable ''horns of Elfland, faintly blowing.'' Then, a ghostly passenger, I have taken my seat in a phantom train, and sped up, up, through the map, rehearsing the journey bit by bit: through the furnace-lit Midlands, and on till the grey glimmer of dawn showed stone walls in place of hedges, and masses looming up on either side; till the bright sun shone upon brown leaping streams and purple heather, and the clear, sharp northern air streamed in through the windows. Return, indeed, was bitter; Endymion-like, "my first touch of the earth went nigh to kill": but it was only to hurry northwards again on the wings of imagination, from dust and heat to the dear mountain air. "We are only the children who might have been," murmured Lamb's dream-babes to him; and for the sake of those dream-journeys, the journeys that might have been, I still hail with a certain affection the call of the engine in the night: even as I love sometimes to turn the enchanted pages of the railway A B C, and pass from one to the other name reminiscent or suggestive of joy and freedom, Devonian maybe, or savouring of Wessex, or bearing me away to some sequestered reach of the quiet Thames.

9

"The Homecoming"

The final two chapters of *The Wind in the Willows*, "Like Summer Tempests came his Tears" and "The Return of Ulysses", were almost wholly conjured up by Kenneth Grahame as he painstakingly brought his masterpiece to its satisfactory and happy ending. There appear to have been no earlier essays from which he obtained his inspiration, although as elsewhere in the book there were experiences from his past upon which he drew. Two of these aspects were the subject of essays he wrote late in his life, and as neither have been in print for a great many years, they demand a place in this book.

The essays, "Fun o' the Fair" and "Oxford through a Boy's Eyes", were among the last works to come from his pen, and both were written at what was to prove his final home, Church Cottage at Pangbourne, to which he had moved from the big Tudor farmhouse at Blewbury, Boham's, in 1924. Unlike Blewbury, which was on the Berkshire Downs, Pangbourne nestled by the River Thames, and was on a direct route to Oxford. Its greatest attraction for Kenneth Grahame, however, was a splendid garden in which he could while away his hours, as well as the fact that the river was just a three minute walk away. Nothing could have been more appropriate than that the man who had found the inspiration to create one of the great works of modern English literature from this river bank, should return to it to see out the last years of his life. For himself, he sought no more than the peace and contentment which he had bestowed at the end of his story on Mole, Rat, Badger and Toad once they had regained Toad Hall from its unlawful occupiers.

Life on the open road had, we know, fascinated Grahame for many years, and gipsies and gipsy caravans, travelling fairs and showmen, would always catch his eye and halt him on a walk. This interest found its way into *The Wind in the Willows* in the shape of Toad's ill-fated caravanning episode, as well as in his bargaining with the gipsy over his horse. But he returned to the topic again in 1925 when he wrote an introduction to the memoirs of ''Lord'' George Sanger entitled *Seventy Years a Showman*. Apart from being one of the most substantial pieces he had written since his novel, it was also a nostalgic and almost wistful piece. Read today, it still comes across as full of the magic spell of caravans and country fairs, and provides us with fresh insights into another corner of Grahame's world, as well as harking back to his great story.

''Oxford through a Boy's Eyes'' is somewhat reminiscent of the final pages of *The Wind in the Willows*, for just as Toad ultimately returns to his ancestral home, so Kenneth Grahame made the return journey to Oxford where he had been a schoolboy in the 1860s. In fact, during the closing years of his life he made frequent trips to Oxford, as his biographer Patrick Chalmers has told us: ''Pangbourne is not far from Oxford, and to Oxford, always dearly loved, Kenneth Grahame would go to enjoy a fair or market, or, *laudator acti*, to decry the cut of the modern undergraduate's trousers, to poke about in Gothic corners, to purchase the latest necktie for his personal wearing.''

That the city was deeply imprinted on his consciousness long before this time is beyond dispute, for writing in 1896 he confessed, ''I constantly at night ran down to a fairy Oxford – the real thing, yet transformed, and better, because the Gothic was better – a maze of lovely cloisters and chapels and courts. I used to spend a long day there and come back next morning. At the end of those ten years (about 1885), I happened to revisit the real Oxford several weeks in succession – I spent several weekends there – and at once the fairy Oxford vanished, and is only just beginning to return now when I have not seen the real thing for

*The churchyard of St. Cross (Holywell), Oxford, where
Kenneth Grahame is buried.*

two years. I like the fairy one better:''* Here, again, with this talk of magical worlds just beneath the surface of the real one, are the self-same feelings that he injected into *The Wind in the Willows*.

''Oxford through a Boy's Eyes'' was to prove Kenneth Grahame's final work, and it was not, in fact, published until after his death, in the December 1932 issue of *Country Life*. His agent had hoped that he might write his autobiography, and although Grahame showed no immediate interest in the task, the fact that he composed this essay indicates that he might have continued his reminiscences beyond his boyhood days had time permitted. But time did not.

Kenneth Grahame died peacefully in his sleep at Church Cottage early on the morning of July 6, 1932. The funeral service took place three days later in Pangbourne, after which his body was most suitably laid to rest in Oxford in Holywell Church-yard. Above his grave was placed an epitaph which perfectly reflected the man, his inspiration and his unique creation:

> To the beautiful memory of Kenneth Grahame, husband
> of Elspeth and father of Alastair, who passed the River on
> the 6th July, 1932, leaving childhood and literature
> through him the more blest for all time.

*   *   *

---

* Fairies were another of Kenneth Grahame's great fascinations, and references to the world of *Faery* dot the pages of *The Wind in the Willows*. One of his closest friends, Graham Robertson, has explained how deep-rooted this interest was: ''Another tie was our mutual interest in Fairyland,'' he wrote, ''upon the manners and customs of which country we could both speak with authority; and we would discuss the points of view, pro-clivities and antecedents of its inhabitants with all the passionate earnestness displayed by really sensible people when speaking of the Latest Quotations, Lunch Scores or Cup Finals. For us the Folk of Fairy Tale were genuine historical characters, and we always tried to enter sympathetically into their feelings, but I remember that we sometimes found the morals of the virtuous heroes and heroines, though much insisted upon, not a little complicated and perplexing.'' This interest apparently went back as far as Kenneth Grahame's days at Oxford when he had fled from the harshness of his school to seek refuge in the fields beyond the town. There he had first encountered the little folk, he explained in an essay entitled ''The Fairy Wicket'', published in the *National Observer* in February 1892, which is reprinted in the Appendix. It is yet another example of Grahame's youthful consciousness moving towards an understanding of the world of nature which was to make *The Wind in the Willows* unique.

FUN O' THE FAIR

THE townsman does not quite realise all the signs and tokens by which the country-dweller knows that the year has really turned, that spring has thrown out its advancing pickets, and that the main forces of summer are well on their way. He knows, indeed, that we hail, each in their turn, the thrust of the snowdrop and then the crocus, the first green thrill that passes over the quickset hedgerows, the tender wash of faint water-colour that tells of the winter wheat now thrusting through, the touch of rosiness in the black elm tree-tops; but perhaps he does not know that one of the truest signs of approaching summer to us is when a sort of frozen Neva in his own suburbs thaws and breaks up, and the flood of caravans that have been winter-bound there is let loose at last – caravans that are to make the little village fairs of the countryside; simple little fairs that nevertheless mean so very much to us.

In a hedgeless country of high downland, on a road that came flowing down, a long white ribbon, straight as it were out of the eastern sky, we would watch, each succeeding spring, for the first appearance of these fairy cruisers of the road. Of course the earliest comers were not for us humble villagers. These would ''open'' at the larger provincial towns, and then start on the circuit they had each planned out for themselves, and we should have to wait our turn, having a couple of nights thrown to us, or perhaps three, if the dates in *Old Moore's Almanac* allowed of it. (''Old Moore'' is the *locus classicus* for the dates of country fairs, so most farmers keep it on their mantel-piece.) But when at last we caught sight of a certain small yellow caravan, with pretty Mrs. S. and the latest baby sitting in front, her husband (who had charge of the dart-throwing department) walking at the horse's head, then we knew that our turn had come at last! ''Enter Autolycus singing!'' For close on the yellow caravan would surely come the larger one, with father and mother and the cooking utensils; and then that other which held Mrs. S.'s three comely young sisters, whom we knew as the Princesses, each, though so young, already a specialist of some sort, and who all slept in one broad bed placed across the rear of their caravan, looking, I should imagine, like three little St. Ursulas by Carpaccio. Later the swing-boats and the wooden horses would straggle in, and all the paraphernalia of the stalls and booths, and the horses (not the wooden ones, of course) would be led away and picketed. Then perhaps, beside a late camp fire, time would be found to renew acquaintance and hear all the news of the past winter; for the winters, to the women at least, were by no means a period of suspended animation.

One does not, it seems, when autumn is over, desert one's caravan for humdrum bricks and mortar. One camps, by arrangement with someone or other, on some piece of waste land or only partly used builder's yard or undeveloped building site on the outskirts of London itself, or of the big new towns, but lately villages themselves, that have sprung up as dormitories to the great city; and there, through all weathers, through rain and frost and snow, one sticks it out in one's little wooden caravan. This may sound very poor fun; but the actual fact was far otherwise. These girls were at first quite strangely reluctant to enlarge upon the joys of a leisured winter life in the neighbourhood of a large city. The reason for this only transpired later, and showed a quite charming delicacy of feeling on their part. ''We thought,'' they explained in effect, ''that it would make you dissatisfied with your hard lot as compared with ours, and perhaps you would be feeling jealous and discontented. For you live in this poky remote little village all the year round, and see nothing and know nothing, and never even guess at all the glamour and excitement that more fortunately placed classes such as ours are free to enjoy.'' We meekly admitted our social disadvantages, but pressed to be allowed a peep at urban life and its glories; and by degrees heard all about the jolly excursions to town, after the train with the black-coated city men had departed, the visits to Parks, Piccadillies, Regent Streets; the studies of shop-windows, and all the ladies' frocks; then bun-shops, matineés, more bun-shops, and a first-class performance at some West End theatre; finally the rush for the last train back, the sleepy journey down, the tramp along a muddy lane and across a field or two to the little caravan at last, making a blacker spot against the dull winter sky; and then the cheerful dazzle of the reflector-lamp on the wall, the cup of cocoa and snack of supper, and laughter and sense of snugness; and so bed at last, St. Ursula-wise, in the little cabin that was all their very own.

Indeed, the show-people are a contented folk, chiefly, I think, because they rarely want to be anything but what they are. They like the life for itself, not for its gains and profits. They generally seem to have enough money, if not a great superfluity. Some people seem to have a vague idea of travelling show-folk as living in Rembrandt interiors on a Salvator Rosa background, in a scene of perpetual high lights and fuliginous shadows full of flashing eyes, tangled gipsy locks, dirt, confusion, clamour and picturesqueness. They are instead a quiet and reserved people, subdued in manner, clannish, living a life apart; scrupulously clean and tidy, as indeed anyone must be who lives in a caravan; self-reliant, asking little from anyone except some tolerance from officials and freedom to come and go and offer their simple wares; and you rarely find a gipsy among them. They intermarry among themselves, and are very proud of their descent from some bygone Champion Sword-swallower or Queen of the Tight-rope; success, if it comes to them, is but modest, reckoned in terms of money; failure means that they are down and out, and there will be no one waiting to help them, except perhaps their own folk.

I have said they are a contented people, and so they are, especially the elders. But among the younger ones, as is natural enough, a little breeze blowing from the land of What-might-have-been will sometimes stir and rustle the leaves of contemplative thought. The Princesses told us they had another married sister, and that *she* lived in a house with a real doorstep, which she could whiten, twice a day if she liked! ''But,'' we protested, ''look at the beautiful steps of your own caravan! Real mahogany, with brass finishings, and hook off and on with a touch!'' ''Yes, but you can't *whiten* them,'' sighed the Princesses wistfully. ''And, besides,'' they added, ''*she* has a permanent address!'' They went on to confess that when the time came for them to think of marriage too, they intended to aim very high – to aim even at a permanent address and a doorstep that could be whitened! Such are the rash dreams of youth! But it is good to carry an ideal about with you, however unattainable it be; and, as R. L. Stevenson has it, to travel hopefully (and in a caravan too!) is better than to arrive (even at a whiteable doorstep).

These girls, by the way, wore the long, tight-waisted corsets in which the fisher-girls, and factory-girls too, of Boulogne so delight the eye. And within the last few weeks I have encountered young gipsy women on the road in just the same type of corset. It was a real pleasure to see it again, with its touch of old-world-liness and even of dignity. If a Paris dressmaker can be imagined visiting a Berkshire common, she might be tempted to try a revision of next season's fashions, and give us an outline once more – if it was only, like Mr. Mantalini's dowager's, a demd outline.

Talking of caravan steps, which are really short ladders, almost perpendicular and without handrail, these have a special influence on the development of the caravan child. For the caravan-born infant, as soon as it can notice anything at all, is swift to detect the contrast between his own cabin'd, cribb'd, confined surroundings and the wonderful great world he catches a glimpse of through the little door – a world consisting of a mighty green common, dotted with white geese plucking at the grass of it, and horses and donkeys tethered here and there, and Daddy and other gods passing freely to and fro. But alas! between you and it stretches a mighty cliff, down which a dizzy ladder crawls! Well, what of it? Such things have got to be tackled sooner or later. So as soon as it can roll or wriggle, and certainly before it can walk, the caravan-infant is down that ladder, somehow, and in due course up it again, and no one knows how it does it, because they are too busy to notice, and they wouldn't interfere if they did in any case, and it never falls, and wouldn't in the least mind if it did.

Few things, I think, are more permanent than the amusements that go to make up a country fair. Changes, of course, come along in time, but they are slow, and more in the nature of adaptations and improvements than revolutions. I suppose the most eternal

feature of a fair is the Roundabout. As the highest expression of
the emotion of joy, we would all of us naturally choose to spring
upon a charger and ride forth at top speed into the boundless
prairie. As we can hardly do that and yet be back in time for tea,
we go round and round and shut our eyes at intervals, trying to
imagine that we are travelling as straight as a cannonball. And if
the horse must needs be of wood, at least it is steady and demands
small skill from its rider. I will here ask connoisseurs of this form
of *haute école* to note that in the best circles such horses have
their names painted on their necks, and that these names are
never invented; they are all the names of very real horses of old
time, taken from some official studbook or other. This ought to
add an interest to every ride, in a real sportsman. Once I had the
fortune to bestride the mighty Eclipse himself, in wooden effigy;
and what gave that ride its special touch of romance was, that it
was in a small provincial town but a few miles from the very place
where that peerless horse was foaled. Only a day or two before I
had walked over the now desolate spot on the edge of the downs.
Wheeled over by plover and played upon by rabbits, only some
slight irregularities of the turf that now covered the site told
where once a great house stood.

The English public is faithful in the main to horses, and does
not greatly care to ride a bear or an ostrich. Pink pigs with blue
ribbons round their necks, so popular in France, where the whole
roundabout will consist of placid pink pigs, I have never met in
England, though there are few more pleasing sights than M. le
Maire, M. le Notaire, and the rest of the principal inhabitants of a
small French town, clad in straw hats, long black frockcoats, and
yellow boots well turned up at the toes, gravely circling round,
each on the back of the pinkest and shiniest of pigs. The great
farmyard cock, again, crested and open-beaked, with wings outstretched and one brawny, scaly leg flung far behind him, is not
so usual as in France – which perhaps is natural. It is the old
English instinct to bestride a horse and not a griffin.

But horses must give way, in shows as elsewhere, to the march
of time, and dummy motor-cars have long challenged the
supremacy of Eclipse and his mates. Children, I think, prefer

them, because they can grasp the dummy steering-wheel and pretend they are driving. And pretend they do, most earnestly. And now to the cars has succeeded a new thing, the chairoplane, which assuredly has come to stay. This fairy thing, with its bird-like undulations, its rushes and its tarryings, is as attractive to look upon as (I should imagine) to form a part of. It is a pretty sight, on some ancient village green, while the upper sky still holds the waning daylight, and the flares are lighting up over the ground below, to see a dozen village maidens, with the silk stockings, scanty skirts and shingled heads that were denied their less emancipated mothers of my own youth, flying with the motion of doves far above one's head. As the poet has it,

> Although I enter not,
> Yet round about the spot
> Oft-times I hover!

As one stands at gaze the daylight slowly wanes, the yellower flares begin to take charge of the atmosphere, the organ brays and the speed increases, and the fluttering riders swing out horizontally in the most bewitching of poses; then sink languidly, droopingly, to rest and earth, and the spell is broken.

Next to the roundabouts must surely be ranked the swing-boats, that tear the insides out of you at the top of every ascent; beloved of the younger and more daring sort, because there seems always just a ghost of a chance that by an extra hard pull one may succeed in completing the revolution and looping the loop. And then we come to another class of sport altogether, the coco-nut throwing, ring-throwing, dart-throwing, all for some very small chance of winning a prize. Some joy in one's skill as a Discobolus may enter into these sports, but the real inspiring motive is the gambler's. Indeed these poor little wooings of fortune may be said to have atrophied down from the full-blooded days when fairs, and especially racecourses, had their gambling-booths open to all and free of interference, each with its tempting piles of gold and silver displayed on its long table. To sum up, then, it may be roughly said that the joys of a fair range themselves under two heads – the delight of exhilarating motion; the excitement of an element of gamble, however trumpery the possible reward.

Perhaps the greatest change that has taken place in show-life in our generation is the disappearance of freaks and monstrosities; and this, it will surely be agreed by all, is a change entirely for good. Of old, freaks were the mainstay of every show. The first fair of importance that I ever attended – I was ten years old at the time – was that of St. Giles's, at Oxford, and I seem to recollect that giants, dwarfs, fat ladies, tattooed ladies, mermaids, six-legged calves and distorted nature of every variety formed the backbone of the show. These have now passed away, and the public taste no longer demands to be disgusted. It must be twenty years since I saw even so much as a fat lady, and that was far down in the West Country, where traditions linger and preferences die hard. Although a printed notice informed you that this mountain of flesh was so genuine throughout that any lady in the audience was permitted, nay invited, to test by pinching, though gentle-men, in the interest of good manners, were kindly requested to refrain; and though a biographical pamphlet related, *inter alia,* that Madame Aurelia's bulk entirely forbade her travelling by train, and a special two-horse van had therefore to be kept at her disposal, yet one could not help feeling uneasily, as one gazed in awe, that there was something wanting. A day or two later, having taken my place in a third-class compartment of a local train, I was greatly pleased when Madame Aurelia – in mufti of course – hopped in as lightly as a bird. We were already five a side, but Madame Aurelia's arrival did not seem to affect our density particularly. She was an amusing woman, and was the life and soul (if hardly the body) of the company, who could not know of course – for there was really nothing to tell them – that they were entertaining such an angel unawares. Illusion, as the show-man knows, is nearly everything.

But I have sometimes reflected since, that my cheerful acquaintance of the railway carriage had possibly been under-studying the real Madame Aurelia, and that on that occasion we had all been "spoofed." Verily the showman hath need of "spoof" as well as illusion. As in the famous picture of Garrick between Tragedy and Comedy, the showman walks between Spoof and Illusion, hand in hand with both.

Yet freaks may still linger on, here and there; but I have not seen a real freak-collection since the days of Barnum, who rather specialised in freaks and always put them in the forefront of his shows. But Barnum, though a great showman, was a bit behind the times, on this side of the water at least. Freaks were already becoming *démodés* when he brought his lot over here though his freaks were good freaks. I can still remember his Fat Lady, who was not only quite reasonably fat but both young and pretty, which of course is not in the bond. I have called her reasonably fat, for I do not think I have ever seen in any show what I would call a *really* fat lady. Elsewhere, perhaps, but not in a show.

The travelling freak-van of old had its contents concealed behind a painted canvas, covering the whole front and depicting the object within under conditions and in surroundings hardly quite realisable, one was tempted to think, within the limitations of a caravan. There mermaids combed their hair on rocks, or swam lazily about in warm tropic seas; there boa constrictors wound themselves round the bodies of paralysed Indian maidens, in the depth of Amazonian jungles. Were it a giant who lurked within, a troop of Lifeguardsmen, helmeted and plumed, rode far below his outstretched arm; while elsewhere the mighty African lion strewed the sand with the dismembered fragments of a hundred savages. All this I absorbed somewhat disconsolately, at my first St. Giles's Fair, wandering sadly down the row of painted booths; for my private means would not allow of a closer acquaintance with the interiors, and so I was obliged in imagination to swim in golden lagoons and wander through parrot-haunted jungles which I was not fated to reach in the flesh. Perhaps after all I had the best of the bargain; for even I could not help noticing, after a while, that the audiences remained within for a remarkably short time, considering all the glories that awaited them there, and that when they came out there was on all their faces what the *Brer Rabbit* book calls "a spell ob de dry grins," showing that they had been well "spoofed" and knew it.

And in fact the whole thing was unabashed "spoofery" – clumsy fakes, dried fish, abortions in bottles, mangy and sickly animals cooped in packing-cases, and so on.

It is to the Cinema that much of this wholesome change in the public taste is due. Few fairs of any size are now without an excellent cinema, where we country folk get the stuff we really like – that is, something as far removed as possible from the quiet and somewhat eventless life we lead. Nature studies and the like may appeal to a jaded London audience; we would fain be, for the fleeting moment, something rather slightly different from our daily selves – say a New York millionaire in love with an Indian half-breed; or a lovely heroine, one moment dancing a two-step in a vast and glittering hall thronged with rank and fashion, the next, without even an audible click, being swept down foaming rapids, raising an appealing, be-diamonded hand to heaven, and wearing, strangely enough, three times as much clothing as she ever appears in on dry land. We like – indeed we prefer – when we call on our stockbroker to buy a hundred Rubbers, to find him stretched on the floor with a bowie-knife through his chest and to be ourselves arrested for the murder. We like it because it is not exactly the sort of life we daily lead; and as we stroll homeward across the starlit common towards our farmhouse, vicarage, or simple thatched cottage, we think "I wish – oh, *how* I wish – I had married an Indian half-breed!"

*   *   *

OXFORD THROUGH A BOY'S EYES

THE main difficulty that confronts me in setting down these random recollections of a now very distant past is to avoid the excursuses, the tempting bypaths, that start into sight and appeal to me at every step of my progress. For instance, I tried to begin in brisk and strictly historical fashion by stating that on or about Michaelmas Day, 1868, a bright and eager (sullen, reluctant, very ordinary-looking) youth of nine summers sprang lightly (descended reluctantly, was hauled ignominiously) on to the arrival platform of the Great Western Railway Station at Oxford; and at once I am arrested by those magic words Railway Station.

Can anything be more eternally immutable than Oxford Station? Paris, Berlin, Vienna, have built, and re-built, and built again, their monumental stations. Hundreds of feet below the surface of London, stations have sporadically spread after the manner of mushroom spawn. I have even lived to see Waterloo Station reconstructed and re-built. But Oxford Station never varies and today is exactly as it flashed upon my eager vision in '68. That it has been re-painted since then I know, for I was once staying in Oxford when this happened, and used to go specially to gaze at the man told off for the job, and admire his deliberate brushwork and the lingering care with which he would add a touch and then step back to admire it. But even then, when he had at last done, the station looked exactly as before.

What a tribute this is to the station itself and its designer! Had there been anything needed to achieve perfection, this, of course, would have been added long ago. But nothing has ever been added, so nothing can have been needed, and Oxford Station, in its static perfection, will be there to greet him as now, when the proverbial stranger comes to gaze on ruins of Christ Church from a broken arch of Folly Bridge.

But we must be getting on. Our hero then, still under the feminine control he was about to quit for the first time, was propelled into – what? – why, a fly, of course, for there was nothing else to be propelled into or by. All England at that period lay fly-blown under the sky, and flies crawled over its whole surface. Whatever station you arrived at, a fly crawled up to you and then crawled off with you. Oxford flies were no worse than other people's – a fly must not be confused with a growler or four-wheeler, though of course it had four wheels all right – flies were solid and roomy and had often seen better days in private service. Some years later, however, there descended on Oxford an extraordinarily shabby collection of what must have been the worst and oldest hansoms ever seen. What town had scrapped and passed them on to us I never knew. It could not have been

London, because the beautiful "Shrewsbury Talbot" type, which revolutionised the London street, had not yet been designed. Aeons passed, however, and these unspeakable survivals crumbled into dust, such fragments as archæologists could preserve being deposited in the Ashmolean alongside the dodo and Guy Fawkes's lantern; and at last, to make amends, Heaven sent Oxford hansoms that were clean, smart and pleasant to look on: cane or straw-coloured, upholstered in light grey, suggesting jinrickshaws, skiffs, anything both swift and cheerful to look at: and these endured until historic times – until, in fact, the advent of the all-devouring taxi.

But this will never do. We haven't even started. On, then, my noble steed (a Tartar of the Ukraine breed). Past the castellated County Buildings, which a young friend of mine once, being up for the first time and bound for the House, mistook for Christ Church and insisted on being deposited there; past (on the other side) the ugly and quite uninteresting church of St. Something-Le-Baily, long ago swept away and replaced by a little public garden: a sharp turn to the left, and New Inn Hall Street burst on the enraptured view.

People who gaze on New Inn Hall Street as it now is must not imagine that things were always just so. On the left, or west side, first you had the buildings composing the Hall itself – the "Tavern" of Verdant Green's days, where the buttery was open all day; then, the grounds and solid Georgian vicarage of St. Something-Le-Baily aforesaid – a pleasant jumble. On the right or east side were little two-storeyed white gabled houses, of the sort common enough in Oxford then, and of which a few specimens still remain, running up to the old fifteenth century back gate of Frewen Hall. Then came St. Edwards, a stone-built mansion of two storeys, reaching to the end and then "returned," as architects say, for its own depth and a trifle over. While the "flyman" is being paid, let us briefly polish off the rest of New Inn Hall Street.

There was no opening through into George Street then. The street turned at a right angle and ran right up to the "Corn", this "leg" being now christened St. Michael's Street. Lodging-houses, and a few private residences, one of which was soon to be taken over by the School for Headmaster's quarters, Oratory, and a bedroom or two, made up the rest of it. Altogether a pleasant, quiet street, central and yet secluded.

Mr. Simeon once told me that he could never find out anything about the house's previous history. Although Oxford climate and Oxford stone had worked together to give it the characteristic of all Oxford stone-built houses older than a certain date, I fancy it must have been a little late for the antiquarian. Quite roughly I should date it at about Queen Anne. One entered by a pleasant low wide hall, recessed to one side, on which lay the then Headmaster's sitting-room, soon to become a senior classroom. To the right, one passed through a low but well lighted eastward-facing room used as a dining-room and supplied with trestle tables, at the head of each of which during meals sat a "Big Boy" (there was no "Sixth" in those troglodytic days). We neophytes were always placed next to one of these great men, the idea being that they would watch over our table manners and deportment – "the juniors, Mr. Weller, is so very savage" – and the theory seems a sound one, always supposing that the Big Boy has any manners himself.

Through the dining-room again, and completing the building in that direction, lay the School Room, a handsome room of some style, running up the full height of the building to a coved ceiling, such ornamentation as it had being classical and "period". I suggest that it may have been of rather later date than the rest, and that the designer may have had in mind a music room. But this, of course, is mere conjecture. Here were desks, allotted to our private ownership, and it also served as a general playroom when we were "confined to barracks". And hence one emerged, by swing doors, into the playground.

This must have been, at one time, a pleasant garden, running north for the whole length of the house and bordered eastwards by the wall of its neighbour, Frewen Hall. Perhaps there were trees in it then, and there still remained, in the receding "waist" of the house, under the dining-room window, some scanty flower-beds, where the horticulturally minded were allowed, and even encouraged, to employ their grovelling instincts. The rest was gravel, with one or two gymnastic appliances. Northwards from the entrance hall, one master's room (I think), the staircase, and then kitchen, pantry, and other offices; rambling, stone-flagged, in the ancient manner. Some sort of stable or garden gateway gave issue on the street northwards; but this was never used, and I only happen to remember it because on my first Guy Fawkes Day we boys attempted a private bonfire, thinking, in our artless way, that in Oxford bonfires were the rule rather than the exception. The authorities, however, thought otherwise, and firemen and police battered at the stable gate aforesaid till explanations ensued and till, I suppose, somebody was squared as usual.

Upstairs, I recall little. It was rabbit-warrenish, and we were distributed in bedrooms, five or six or thereabouts apiece. There was also a master's sitting-room, a cheerful bow-windowed room overlooking the playground. Thither I was shortly summoned, and met a round and rosy young man with side-whiskers, who desired, he said, to record my full name for some base purpose of his own. When he had got it he tittered girlishly, and murmured "What a *funny* name!" His own name was – but there! I think I won't say what his own name was. I merely mention this little incident to show the sort of stuff we bright lads of the late 'sixties sometimes found ourselves up against.

A more painful incident occurred a day or two later. The lowest class, or form, was in session, and I was modestly lurking in the lower end of it wondering what the deuce it was all about, when enter the Headmaster. He did not waste words. Turning to the master in charge of us, he merely said: "If *that*" (indicating my shrinking figure) "is not up *there*" (pointing to the upper strata) "by the end of the lesson, he is to be caned." Then like a blast away he passed, and no man saw him more.

Here was an affair! I was young and tender, well meaning, not used to being clubbed and assaulted; yet here I was, about to be savaged by big, beefy, hefty, hairy men, called masters! Small wonder that I dissolved into briny tears. It was the correct card to play in any case, but my emotion was genuine. Yet what happened? Not a glance, not a word, was exchanged; but my gallant comrades, one and all, displayed an ignorance, a stupidity, which, even for them, seemed to me unnatural. I rose, I soared, till, dazed and giddy, I stood at the very top of the class; and there my noble-hearted colleagues insisted on keeping me until the peril was past, when I was at last allowed to descend from that "bad eminence" to which merit had certainly never raised me. What maggot had tickled the brain of the Headmaster on that occasion I never found out. Schoolmasters never explain, never retract, never apologise.

Of course, the canings came along all right, in due time. But after I had seen my comrades licked, or many of them, the edge of my anticipation was somewhat dulled.

We used to play cricket under difficulties on Port Meadow (this must have been in the following year). The sole advantage of Port Meadow as a cricket pitch was the absence of boundaries. If an ambitious and powerful slogger wanted to hit a ball as far as Wolvercote, he could do so if he liked; there was nothing to stop him, and the runs would be faithfully run out. The chief drawback was that the city burgesses used the meadow for pasturage of their cows – graminivorous animals of casual habits. When fielding was "deep", and frenzied cries of "Throw her up!" reached one from the wicket, it was usually more discreet to feign a twisted ankle or a sudden faintness, and allow some keener enthusiast to recover the ball from where it lay.

But this expeditionary sort of big-game hunting ceased, so far as cricket was concerned, when we got the use of the White House cricket ground, since devoted to the baser uses of "Socker" on half-holidays. This was a satisfactory and well kept little ground, and I never remember any complaints about it. How football fared I entirely forget.

Now for what I may call our extra-mural life, apart from games. During lawful hours we were free to wander where we liked, and it was my chief pleasure to escape at once and foot it here and there, exploring, exploring, always exploring, in a world I had not known the like of before. And when I speak of footing it, I am reminded that pious pilgrims now visit Merton Street to gaze on the only survival of the cobblestone or kidney paving of mediævalism; but in the time I speak of, most of the Oxford streets were as cobbled as Merton. The High, to be sure, was macadam, and no trams yet squealed their way down its length to a widened Magdalen Bridge. But the Broad was all cobble, so, I fancy, was St. Giles, and most of the lesser streets, including Brasenose Lane.

Why I "drag in" Brasenose Lane, like Velazquez, at this particular point, is that I have reason to remember its cobbles well. We loved to pass with beating hearts along that gloomy *couloir*, pause on its protuberant cobbles, and point out to each other the precise window behind which, on that fatal Sunday night, the members of the Hell Fire Club (Oxford branch) were holding their unhallowed orgies when the blackest sinner of the crew expired on the floor in strong convulsions, while, outside, a strayed reveller was witness of the Devil himself, horned and hoofed and of portentous stature, extracting the wretched man's soul slowly through the bars, as a seaside tripper might extract a winkle from its shell with a pin. There was always a thrill waiting for you in that little street; and though much of its terror has passed away, especially since they asphalted it, I should not much like, even at this day, to pass along Brasenose Lane at midnight.

I said just now that we were free to wander where we liked; but there were "bounds", mystic but definite, and these we never overstepped – first, because it was so easy for us to be spotted in our school caps, and secondly, because we didn't want to. These bounds chiefly excluded districts like St. Ebbes, St. Thomas's (except for church), the Cattle Market, Jericho, and their like, and there was little temptation to go exploring in such quarters. One result, however, of these bounds has been, in my own case, slightly comical. Though before I was ten I knew all the stately buildings that clustered round the Radcliffe Library like my own pocket, as the French say, it was only in comparatively recent times that I even set eyes on Paradise Square or looked upon the Blue Pig in Gloucester Green. And even as I write these words I hear rumours that the Blue Pig, like so much that is gone or going, is threatened with demolition. This seems to be a case for one of our modern poets to speak the word and avert the doom. Browning once wrote a poem which (he said) was to save the Paris Morgue from a similar fate – though I don't think he succeeded in doing so. Please, Mr. Masefield of Boar's Hill, will you not save us our Blue Pig?

Two things struck me forcibly when I began my explorations. The first was the exceeding blackness of the University buildings, which really seemed to my childish mind as if it was intentional, and might have been put on with a brush, in a laudable attempt to produce the "sub-fusc" hue required in the attire of its pupils. Of course, one must remember that in those days there was not so much of the architectural "spit and polish" that now goes on during the Long. A man could then go down in June with the assurance that he would find much the same Oxford awaiting him when he returned in the autumn. Now it is otherwise, though the climate sees to it that in a term or two things are much as before.

Perhaps the things most remarkable at that time for their exceeding nigritude and decay were the Sheldonian Cæsars. Those who now pause to study their (comparatively) clean-cut features can form little idea of the lumps of black fungoid growth they once resembled. It is the original Cæsars I am referring to, of course – not the last set – a comparatively fresh and good-looking lot. In the closing words of "A Soul's Tragedy" the speaker observes: "I have known *four* and twenty leaders of revolution." Well I have known *three* sets of Sheldonian Cæsars: and perhaps, with luck, I shall yet know a fourth.

The Sheldonian should really be more careful of its Cæsars. It uses them up so fast – almost as fast as old Rome herself did. There must be some special reason for it. Perhaps it is the English pronunciation of the Latin in which the Public Orations are delivered. No patriotic and self-respecting Cæsars could be expected to stand that – and they don't. They flake, they peel, they wilt, in dumb protest. Or can it be the Latin itself? But no, that would be unthinkable.

The other most abiding impression that I then received was from the barred windows, the massive, bolted and enormous gates, which every college had, which were never used or opened, and which gave these otherwise hospitable residences the air of Houses of Correction. The window-bars, of course, were not the chief puzzle. The Mid-Victorian young were dangerous animals, only existing on sufferance, and kept as far as possible behind bars, where one need not be always sending to see what baby is doing and tell him not to. The porter's lodge system also has much to say for itself. But those great and lofty double gates, sternly barred and never open invitingly, what could they portend? I wondered. It was only slowly and much later that I began to understand that they were strictly emblematical and intended to convey a lesson. Among the blend of qualities that go to make up the charm of collegiate life, there was then more than a touch of – shall I say? – exclusiveness and arrogance. No one thought the worse of it on that account: still, its presence was felt, and the gates stood to typify it. Of course, one would not dream of suggesting that the arrogance may still be there. But the gates remain.

As to the exclusiveness, I have nothing to complain of personally. The only things I wanted to get at were certain gardens, and I never remember being refused entry, though this might very well have happened to a small boy, always such an object of suspicion. It was really better than at home, where, of course, one had friends with beautiful gardens, but they usually meant formal calls and company manners, and perhaps tedious talk of delphiniums and green fly and such. Here, one strolled in when one was in the mood, and strolled out when one had had enough, and no one took the slightest notice of you. It was an abiding pleasure, and to those who made it possible for me I here tender, *ex voto*, my belated thanks.

After the colleges came urban joys, and specially the shops in the High. There were more of these then than now, as Oriel had not "come through", nor had Brasenose emerged into air and light, and both these colleges were shop-eaters. Then there was the market, always a joy to visit. It seemed to have everything the heart of man could desire, from livestock at one end to radiant flowers in pots at the other. It is still one of the pleasantest spots I know, and when I have half an hour to spare in Oxford, or one of her too frequent showers sends me flying to cover, I love to roam its dusky and odorous corridors, gazing longingly at all the good things I am no longer permitted to eat.

Appendix

I

SECRET KINGDOMS

THIS is an over-surveyed age, and rarely now are atlases to be found containing those broad buff spaces so dear to our youth, unbroken by the blue of any lake, crawled upon by no caterpillar mountain ranges; wherein you might rear a dozen clamorous cities of magic, and yet leave room for a prairie or two, a Sahara, and a brand-new set of Rockies. But there are kingdoms yet to discover, and golden realms that await their Marco Polo. Every one of these children, who are going about the business of life so absorbedly, with such small regard for us big fellows coming and going vaguely, out of focus, on the edge of their horizon, has got a particular one of his own, shimmering with barbaric pearl and gold, pleasantly elastic as to its boundaries. You may be quite sure of this; and you may be equally sure of another thing – that you shall never enter in. Whatever the extent of his usual confidences, this gate is sternly shut.

The reason why? Well, perhaps mainly shamefacedness. The thing as seen by him would appear to you, he knows well, too incredibly fantastic. Possibly he would be laughed at – the sort of criminal dock in which a child most dreads to stand. In any case he lacks the language for the task. The expression of the commonest sentiments is apt to gravel him; how much more the voicing of these nebulae – as impossible a business as if he were bidden to sing in colour, or to paint in odours gathered from the garden. But, above all, to reveal would be in some sort to break the spell; and this is his own treasure, his peculiar possession – perhaps the only thing he has got which is altogether and entirely his very own. Even with each other, children do not usually share their kingdoms. To be sure, a fellow-feeling in kingdoms is a rare fine thing – the only thing, perhaps, really worthy the name of sympathy; and kingdoms blossom and expand so splendidly under a judicious dual control. But the risk is too great – the risk of jeers, rebuffs, sheer incapacity to understand – to make such confidences common.

These kingdoms, it should be well understood, are no casual resorts, but exist side by side with the other life evident to the grosser visual rays, occupying at least a fair half of actual existence. At regular periods, the child steps deliberately out of the present tangibility into his property over the border; and again, when his time is up, steps just as deliberately back. In continuity, in ordered procession of facts, the thing goes on with just the same regularity as that other routine of baths, bread-and-butter, lessons and bed; and is about as near a thing to a fourth dimension as can be found in actual working order.

Cases will vary, of course, with dispositions and temperaments. Some wealthy and enviable mites run three or four kingdoms at once, of differing qualities and capabilities, keeping them all going together, as a juggler sustains half a dozen oranges in mid-air. Others there are, of more fickle nature, who periodically abandon their kingdoms for fresh conquests in a newer Spain. The lion and the lizard keep those forgotten courts, wherein they were wont to disport themselves during church-service. The owl hoots and the wind blows chill through those vast buildings of yester-year, a short time since so full of song and laughter. They themselves, forgetful ones, are up and away across the virgin prairies of another land, unrepresented in Europe by any ambassador. But, as a general rule, the kingdom is colonised in the earliest possible days of subconsciousness – undergoes alterations, of course, extensions, re-peoplings, as time goes on and experience teaches lessons – but remains practically the same kingdom, always there, always handy to step into, up to a time when one would blush to be suspected of such a possession. At what specific date indeed, dare one fix the terminus? Cataclysmal periods arrive, and shake us, and pass, and the kingdom endures. There is the fateful moment, for instance, when one "goes into tails''. At school they nip for the first coat-tail. Nips are the direful penalty, and with nips comes much besides. Yet the kingdom often remains, surviving nips, dignities, and responsibilities. Other portentous changes succeed – I will not enumerate them; with which of them can one say the kingdom vanishes? One wakes up some day and finds it gone. Yet who can name the date of the eclipse?

As for the population: your regular relations, whose mistaken adherence to an indefensible scheme of life brings them so frequently into collision with you – they are rarely seen there, and then only in distressingly menial positions. Hewers of wood and drawers of water, all of them, if so be as they have even the luck to get a ticket of admission at all. On the other hand, the casual people who have been kind to you and passed, or have won your heart by athletic or other similar gifts – here they walk as princes and familiars, doing wondrous things, sharing with you the ungrudged sweets of empire. And yet, while the kingdom's chief charm lies in its constancy, in its abiding presence there at your elbow, the smiling gate wide open, whether fortune favour or frown, its inhabitants are sadly apt to vary. Other folk come on the scene, who tip you, and take you to treats, and have to be recognised and considered accordingly; so from time to time, as you revisit the familiar land, fresh guests travel down with you, and fresh heroes make up your house-party. Then there is the Princess – well, honestly I think princesses are more permanent. They change at times, of course, they drop out, they disappear; but it is usually more their fault than yours. They cease to be kind, perhaps they take up with another fellow, or leave your part of the country; and under such circumstances only a novelist would expect you to remain true. Absolute inconstancy, a settled habit of fickleness, belongs, I am sure, to a later period. The Princess, then, often sees out many a guest of real distinction; nay, she is frequently your sole comrade, through storied cities, on desert isles, or helping to handle your cutter where the Southern Cross is reflected in fairy seas. Then it is that you say at your leisure all those fine things that you never can get off through the garden-hedge; while she, for her part, is sympathetic, appreciative and companionable, to a degree you never would guess from the shy awkwardness that masters her in this narrow little world down here. And yet – an embarrassing person somewhat at times. One has often a surmise that she is not being done full justice – in spite of her capacities for pulling an oar or loading a musket, she is meant for better things.

These kingdoms, I have said, are always close at hand, always attainable in case of need. But, of course, there are special periods of vacation, when one resorts thither so habitually that schemes and arrangements can be settled beforehand, to be worked out in detail when the regular hour arrives. The reading aloud of improving matter – something without any story in it – at stated times, may even come to be looked forward to, if you happen to possess a fine, healthy kingdom, in good working order, that requires your attention for a more protracted spell than just between courses at table. A duty-walk with an uninteresting person is simply a return ticket to cloudland. As bed-time arrives you promptly book for the same terminus; hence it comes that you never properly fall asleep in this tangible world, but pass through the stage of your own peculiar country to that droll continent which mixes up your two existences for you with a humour you could never achieve unaided. But the services of the Church afford the most fixed and certain periods of all; for nothing short of a sick bed saves you from the grim compulsion, while, on the other hand, once there, little is asked of you but quiet and conformity to a certain muscular routine. Parents, therefore, should be very modest, when inclined to flatter themselves that the passing thoughts and reflections of their children are quite clear to them, and that they can follow the ripple of every mood on those ingenuous countenances. The mother who notes with delight the rapt, absorbed air of her little son, during the course of a sermon that is stirring her own very vitals, and builds high hopes thereon, is probably egregiously mistaken. Ten to one he is a thousand miles away, safe in his own kingdom; and what is more, he has shut the door behind him. *She* is left outside, with the parson and the clerk.

In the same way, a child who is distraught during the

conversational hour of meals, answering at random or not at all;
who fails to catch the salient points of an arithmetic or geography
lesson – seeming, indeed, to regard these statistics and weary
columns from very far off – is not necessarily a fool, nor half-
baked as to mental equipment. He has probably got a severer task
cut out for him, and has need of all his wits and all his energies.
The expedition he is leading, the palace he is exploring, the
friends he is entertaining with that abandonment so characteristic
of a land without a currency – all these undertakings evoke com-
mendable qualities. Indeed, who shall say he is not educating
himself all the time? In his own way, of course, not yours.

It should always be remembered that whenever a child is set
down in a situation that is distasteful, out of harmony, jarring –
and he is very easily jarred – that very moment he begins,
without conscious effort, to throw out and to build up an
environment really suitable to his soul, and to transport himself
thereto. And there he will stay, of a certainty, until you choose to
make things pleasanter. Life is so rough to him, so full of pricks
and jogs and smartings, that without this blessed faculty of
projecting a watertight skin – nay, an armour-plating – his little
vessel's seams would gape and its timbers crack too early. That
which flows in his veins is ichor, closing the very wounds
through which it issues; and of the herb called self-heal he has
always a shred or two in his wallet.

This mental aloofness of the child – this habit of withdrawal
into a secret chamber, of which he sternly guards the key – may
have been often a cause of disappointment, of some
disheartenment even, to the parent who thinks there can be no
point, no path, no situation, where he cannot be an aid and an
exposition, a guide, philosopher, and friend; more especially to
the one who, by easy but fatal degrees, reaches the point of
desiring to walk in the child's garden as very God, both in the
heat and the cool of his day. Let it be some consolation to them
that they are the less likely to father a prig. This Bird of Paradise
that he carries encaged within him, this Host that he guards
within his robe through the jostling mart of shouting
commonplaces, may be both germ and nutriment of an

individuality which shall at least never suffer him to be a tame replica. The child to despair of is more rightly the one who shall be too receptive, too responsive, too easily a waxy phonograph.

Meantime these kingdoms continue, happily, to flourish and abound. Space is filled with their iridescences, and every fresh day bubbles spring up towards the light. We know it – we know it: and yet we get no nearer them. Perhaps we are, unwittingly, even invited and honoured guests; this is not the sort of invitation we would be likely to refuse. Possibly we may be walking, even now, arm-in-arm with some small comrade of real affinity of spirit, sharing in just those particular absurdities we would most like to commit. And all the time we are trundling about here dully in hansom cabs, while the other one of us, the lucky half, is having *such* a magnificent time! For the current is not yet switched on, the circuit is not yet made complete, by which we shall some day (I trust) have power to respond to these delightful biddings out of town, and get a real change of air, For the present we are helpless. Surely the shouts, the laughter, the banging of guns and the music, make noise enough to reach our ears? Ineffectually we strain and listen: we have lost our key, and are left kicking our heels in the dark and chilly street. And only just the other side of that wall – that wall which we shall never climb – what fun, what revels are going on!

*   *   *

II

NONSENSE-LAND

THERE is a sort of a garden – or rather an estate, of park and fallow and waste – nay, perhaps we may call it a kingdom, albeit a noman's-land and an everyman's land – which lies so close to the frontier of our work-a-day world that a step will take us therein. Indeed, some will have it that we are there all the time, that it is the real fourth dimension, and that at any moment – if we did but know the trick – we might find ourselves trotting along its pleasant alleys, without once quitting our arm-chair. Nonsense-Land is one of the names painted up on the board at the frontier-station; and there the custom-house officers are very strict. You may take as much tobacco as you please, any quantity of spirits, and fripperies of every sort, new and old; but all common-sense, all logic, all serious argument, must strictly be declared, and is promptly confiscated. Once safely across the border, it is with no surprise at all that you greet the Lead Soldier strutting somewhat stiffly to meet you, the Dog with eyes as big as mill-wheels following affably at his heel; on the banks of the streams little Johnny-head-in-air is perpetually being hauled out of the water; while the plaintive voice of the Gryphon is borne inland from the margin of the sea.

Most people, at one time or another, have travelled in this delectable country, if only in young and irresponsible days. Certain unfortunates, unequipped by nature for a voyage in such latitudes, have never visited it at all, and assuredly never will. A happy few never quit it entirely at any time. Domiciled in that pleasant atmosphere, they peep into the world of facts but fitfully, at moments; and decline to sacrifice their high privilege of citizenship at any summons to a low conformity.

Of this fortunate band was Eugene Field. He knew the country thoroughly, its highways and its byways alike. Its language was the one he was fondest of talking; and he always refused to emigrate and to settle down anywhere else. As soon as he set himself to narrate the goings-on there, those of us who had been tourists in bygone days, but had lost our return-tickets, pricked up our ears, and listened, and remembered, and knew. The Dinkey-Bird, we recollected at once, had been singing, the day we left, in the amfalula-tree; and there, of course, he must have been singing ever since, only we had forgotten the way to listen. Eugene Field gently reminded us, and the Dinkey-Bird was vocal once more, to be silent never again. Shut-Eye Train had been starting every night with the utmost punctuality; it was we who had long ago lost our way to the booking-office (I really do not know the American for booking-office). Now we can hurry up the platform whenever we please, and hear the doors slam and the whistle toot as we sink back on those first-class cushions! And the Chocolate Cat, – why, of course the cats were all chocolate then! And how pleasantly brittle their tails were, and how swiftly, though culled and sucked each day, they sprouted afresh!

It is an engaging theory, that we are all of us just as well informed as the great philosophers, poets, wits, who are getting all the glory; only unfortunately our memories are not equally good – we forget, we forget so terribly! Those belauded gentlemen, termed by our fathers ''makers'' – creators, to wit – they are only *reminders* after all: flappers, Gulliver would have called them. The parched peas in their gaily-painted bladders rattle with reminiscences as they flap us on the ears; and at once we recall what we are rightly abashed beyond measure to have for one instant forgotten. At any rate, it is only when the writer comes along who strikes a new clear note, who does a thing both true and fresh, that we say to ourselves, not only ''How I wish I had done that myself!'' – but also ''And I *would* have done it, too – if only I had remembered it in time!'' Perhaps this is one of the tests of originality.

Of course I am touching upon but one side of Eugene Field the writer. An American of Americans, much of his verse was devoted to the celebration of what we may call the minor joys which go to make social happiness in the life he lived with so frank and rounded a completion – a celebration which appealed to his countrymen no less keenly, that the joys were of a sort which, perhaps from some false sense of what makes fitness in subject, had hitherto lacked their poet – on that side at least. This, of course, was the fault of the poets. And though I spoke just now of minor joys, there are really no such things as minor joys – or minor thrushes and blackbirds. Fortunately this other aspect does not need to be considered here. I say fortunately, because it is not given to a writer to know more than one Land – to know it intimately, that is to say, so as to dare to write about it. This is the Law and the Prophets. Even that most native utterance, which sings of ''the clink of the ice in the pitcher that the boy brings up the hall'', appeals to us but faintly, at second-hand. That pitcher does not clink in England.

In this spheral existence all straight lines, sufficiently prolonged, prove to be circles: and a line of thought is no exception. We are back at the point we started from – the consideration of Eugene Field as a citizen; of a sort of a cloud-country, to start with; and later, of a land more elemental. In either capacity we find the same note, of the joy of life. We find the same honest resolve, to accept the rules and to play out the game accordingly; the same conviction, that the game is in itself a good one, well worth the playing. And so, with no misgiving, he takes his America with just the same heartiness as his Nonsense-land.

The little boy who should by rights have been lost in the forest, by the white pebbles he had warily dropped found his way back safely to sunlight and to home; and to keep in touch with earth is at least to ensure progression in temperate and sweet-breathed atmosphere, as well as in a certain zone, and that no narrow one, of appreciation; the appreciation of our fellows, the world over; those who, whatever their hemisphere, daily find themselves pricked by a common sun, with the same stimulus for every cuticle, towards pleasures surprisingly similar.

* * *

III

MR. MOLE'S CHAR-MOUSE

Or, Who cleaned Mole End in the Owner's Absence?

IT may perhaps be pointed out in his defence, that Mole, though unmarried and evidently in rather poor circumstances, as incomes go nowadays, could probably have afforded some outside assistance say twice a week or so; indeed, living as he did, it would be almost a necessity.

He probably then had a Char-Mouse in for a few hours and her dinner on certain days, and the animal would have cleaned up his whitewashing mess in a perfunctory way. Then, finding that her weekly pittance was no longer forthcoming, she quite naturally and properly would have taken her services elsewhere, though from kindness of heart she might have continued to give an occasional eye to the goldfish.

I would ask you to observe that our author practises a sort of "character economy" which has the appearance of being deliberate. The presence of certain characters may be indicated in or required by the story, but if the author has no immediate use for them, he simply ignores their existence.

Take this very question of domestic service – however narrow poor Mole's means may have been, it is evident that Rat was comfortably off – indeed, I strongly suspect him of a butler-rat and cook-housekeeper. Toad Hall, again, must have been simply crawling with idle servants, eating their heads off.

But the author doesn't happen to want them, so for him they simply don't exist. He doesn't say they are *not* there; he just leaves them alone.

To take another instance – the wretched fellow, ignorant as he is, must have known perfectly well that the locomotive on which Toad escaped required the services of a stoker, as well as an engine-driver, but he didn't happen to *want* a stoker, so he simply ignored him.

I think you will find that this same character-economy runs through all the classic old fairy-tales and our author probably thought that he was sinning (if sinning at all) in very good company.

The modern method leaves so little to the imagination of the reader that it describes with insistent particularity the appearance of the taxi-driver who did *not* say "Thank you" to the heroine when she gave him 3d. above the legal fare from South Audley Street to Waterloo.

Our author would have treated a taxi exactly as he would treat a Magic Carpet (which indeed is just what it is) and would not have given the taxi a driver at all! And this is right, for not one passenger in a hundred is ever conscious of the presence of a driver at all.

They only see at the end a paw thrust out into which they drop something, and the taxi vanishes with a snort. Probably Magic

Carpets had drivers, too, but the authors of old saw that they were unessential to their stories, and ignored them.

*   *   *

IV

THE FAIRY WICKET

FROM digging in the sandy, over-triturated soil of times historical, all dotted with date and number and sign, how exquisite the relief in turning to the dear days outside history – yet not so very far off neither for us nurslings of the northern sun – when kindly beasts would loiter to give counsel by the wayside, and a fortunate encounter with one of the Good People was a surer path to Fortune and the Bride than the best-worn stool that ever proved step-ladder to aspiring youth. For then the Fairy Wicket stood everywhere ajar – everywhere and to each and all. "Open, open, green hill!" – you needed no more recondite sesame than that: and, whoever you were, you might have a glimpse of the elfin dancers in the hall that is litten within by neither sun nor moon; or catch at the white horse's bridle as the Fairy Prince rode through. It has been closed now this many a year (the fairies, always strong in the field, are excellent wicket-keepers); and if it open at all, 'tis but for a moment's mockery of the material generation that so deliberately turned its back on the gap into Elf-Land – that first stage to the Beyond.

It was a wanton trick, though, that these folk of malice used to play on a small school-boy, new kicked out of his nest into the draughty, uncomfortable outer world, his unfledged skin still craving the feathers whereinto he was wont to nestle. The barrack-like school, the arid, cheerless class-rooms, drove him to Nature for redress; and, under an alien sky, he would go forth and wander along the iron road by impassive fields, so like yet so unlike those hitherto a part of him and responding to his every mood. And to him, thus loitering with overladen heart, there would come suddenly a touch of warmth, of strange surprise. The

turn of the road just ahead – that, sure, is not all unfamiliar? That
row of elms – it cannot entirely be accident that they range just
so? And, if not accident, then round the bend will come the old
duck-pond, the shoulder of the barn will top it, a few yards on will
be the gate – it swings-to with its familiar click – the dogs race
down the avenue – and then – and then! It is all wildly fanciful;
and yet, though knowing not Tertullian, a *"credo quia
impossibile"* is on his tongue as he quickens his pace – for what
else can he do? A step, and the spell is shattered – all is cruel and
alien once more; while every copse and hedge-row seems a-tinkle
with faint elfish laughter. The Fairies have had their joke: they
have opened the wicket one of their own hand's-breadths, and
shut it in their victim's face. When next that victim catches a
fairy, he purposes to tie up the brat in sight of his own green hill,
and set him to draw up a practical scheme for Village Councils.

One of the many women I ever really loved, fair in the fearless
old fashion, was used to sing, in the blithe, unfettered accent of
the people: "I'd like to be a fairy, And dance upon my toes, I'd
like to be a fairy, And wear short close!" And in later life it is to
her sex that the wee (but very wise) folk sometimes delegate their
power of torment. Such understudies are found to play the part
exceeding well; and many a time the infatuated youth believes he
sees in the depth of one sole pair of eyes – blue, brown, or green
(the fairy colour) – the authentic fairy wicket standing ajar: many
a time must he hear the quaint old formula, "I'm sure, if I've
ever done anything to lead you to think," etc. (runs it not so?),
ere he shall realise that here is the gate upon no magic pleasance
but on a cheap suburban villa, banging behind the wrathful rate-
collector or hurled open to speed the pallid householder to the
Registrar's Office. In still grosser habitations, too, they lurk, do
the People of Mischief, ready to frolic out on the unsuspecting
one: as in the case, which still haunts my memory, of a certain
bottle of an historic Château-Yquem, hued like Venetian glass,
odorous as a garden in June. Forth from out the faint perfume of
this haunted drink there danced a bevy from Old France, clad in
the fashion of Louis-Quinze, peach-coloured knots of ribbon
bedizening apple-green velvets, as they moved in stately wise

among the roses of the old garden, to the quaint music – Rameau, was it? – of a fairy *cornemuse*, while fairy Watteaus, Fragonards, Lancrets, sat and painted them. Alas! too shallow the bottle, too brief the brawls: not to be recalled by any quantity of Green Chartreuse.

Acknowledgements

The Editor would like to thank the staffs of the British Museum, The British Newspaper Library and the London Library for their help in his research and in particular the tracing of the newspapers and periodicals in which Kenneth Grahame's early essays appeared. He also acknowledges with grateful thanks the assistance of W. O. G. Lofts, a researcher of redoubtable tenacity, and Tessa Harrow, for her help in the concept and structure of the book.

The following works were also consulted during the preparation of this book, and grateful acknowledgement is given to the authors and publishers: John Murray for *Kenneth Grahame: A Study of his Life, Work and Times* by Peter Green (1959); The Bodley Head for *Kenneth Grahame* by Eleanor Graham (1963); and Methuen Ltd for *Kenneth Grahame: Life, Letters and Unpublished Work* by Patrick R. Chalmers (1933). Finally, my thanks to Messrs. Curtis Brown as agents for the estate of A. A. Milne, for permission to quote from his introduction to the 1940 edition of *The Wind in the Willows* published by Methuen Ltd.